MONETARY, FISCAL AND TRADE POLICIES

EXCHANGE RATES AND CURRENCY DEBATES

ISSUES IN GLOBAL MONETARY POLICY

MONETARY, FISCAL AND TRADE POLICIES

Additional books in this series can be found on Nova's website
under the Series tab.

Additional E-books in this series can be found on Nova's website
under the E-book tab.

Monetary, Fiscal and Trade Policies

Exchange Rates and Currency Debates

Issues in Global Monetary Policy

Darren Byers
Editor

New York

Copyright © 2013 by Nova Science Publishers, Inc.

All rights reserved. No part of this book may be reproduced, stored in a retrieval system or transmitted in any form or by any means: electronic, electrostatic, magnetic, tape, mechanical photocopying, recording or otherwise without the written permission of the Publisher.

For permission to use material from this book please contact us:
Telephone 631-231-7269; Fax 631-231-8175
Web Site: http://www.novapublishers.com

NOTICE TO THE READER

The Publisher has taken reasonable care in the preparation of this book, but makes no expressed or implied warranty of any kind and assumes no responsibility for any errors or omissions. No liability is assumed for incidental or consequential damages in connection with or arising out of information contained in this book. The Publisher shall not be liable for any special, consequential, or exemplary damages resulting, in whole or in part, from the readers' use of, or reliance upon, this material. Any parts of this book based on government reports are so indicated and copyright is claimed for those parts to the extent applicable to compilations of such works.

Independent verification should be sought for any data, advice or recommendations contained in this book. In addition, no responsibility is assumed by the publisher for any injury and/or damage to persons or property arising from any methods, products, instructions, ideas or otherwise contained in this publication.

This publication is designed to provide accurate and authoritative information with regard to the subject matter covered herein. It is sold with the clear understanding that the Publisher is not engaged in rendering legal or any other professional services. If legal or any other expert assistance is required, the services of a competent person should be sought. FROM A DECLARATION OF PARTICIPANTS JOINTLY ADOPTED BY A COMMITTEE OF THE AMERICAN BAR ASSOCIATION AND A COMMITTEE OF PUBLISHERS.

Additional color graphics may be available in the e-book version of this book.

Library of Congress Cataloging-in-Publication Data

ISBN: 978-1-62948-616-1

Published by Nova Science Publishers, Inc. † New York

CONTENTS

Preface		**vii**
Chapter 1	Current Debates over Exchange Rates: Overview and Issues for Congress *Rebecca M. Nelson*	**1**
Chapter 2	China's Currency Policy: An Analysis of the Economic Issues *Wayne M. Morrison and Marc Labonte*	**41**
Chapter 3	The Depreciating Dollar: Economic Effects and Policy Response *Craig K. Elwell*	**101**
Chapter 4	Currency Manipulation: The IMF and WTO *Jonathan E. Sanford*	**131**
Index		**145**

PREFACE

Exchange rates are important in the international economy, because they affect the price of every country's imports and exports, as well as the value of every overseas investment. Following the global financial crisis of 2008-2009 and ensuing economic recession, disagreements among countries over exchange rates have become more widespread. Some policy leaders and analysts contend that there is a "currency war" now underway among certain countries. At the heart of current disagreements is whether or not countries are using exchange rate policies to undermine free markets and intentionally push down the value of their currency in order to gain a trade advantage at the expense of other countries. A weak currency makes exports cheaper to foreigners, which can lead to higher exports and job creation in the export sector. However, if one country weakens its currency, there can be implications for other countries. In general, exporters and firms producing import-sensitive goods may find it harder to compete against countries with weak currencies. However, consumers and businesses that rely on inputs from abroad may benefit when other countries have weak currencies, because imports may become cheaper. The United States has found itself on both sides of the current debates over exchange rates. This book provides an overview of exchange rate and currency debate issues and global monetary policy.

Chapter 1 - Exchange rates are important in the international economy, because they affect the price of every country's imports and exports, as well as the value of every overseas investment. Following the global financial crisis of 2008-2009 and ensuing economic recession, disagreements among countries over exchange rates have become more widespread. Some policy leaders and analysts contend that there is a "currency war" now underway among certain countries.

At the heart of current disagreements is whether or not countries are using exchange rate policies to undermine free markets and intentionally push down the value of their currency in order to gain a trade advantage at the expense of other countries. A weak currency makes exports cheaper to foreigners, which can lead to higher exports and job creation in the export sector. However, if one country weakens its currency, there can be implications for other countries. In general, exporters and firms producing import-sensitive goods may find it harder to compete against countries with weak currencies. However, consumers and businesses that rely on inputs from abroad may benefit when other countries have weak currencies, because imports may become cheaper.

The United States has found itself on both sides of the current debates over exchange rates. On one hand, some Members of Congress and U.S. policy experts argue that U.S. exports and U.S. jobs have been adversely affected by the exchange rate policies adopted by China, Japan, and a number of other countries. On the other hand, some emerging markets, including Brazil and Russia, have argued that expansionary monetary policies in the United States and other developed countries caused the currencies of developed countries to depreciate, hurting the competitiveness of emerging markets. More recently, however, emerging-market currencies have started to depreciate, and now there are concerns about emerging-market currencies becoming too weak relative to the currencies of some developed economies.

Through the International Monetary Fund (IMF), countries have committed to avoid "currency manipulation." There are also provisions in U.S. law to address "currency manipulation" by other countries. In the context of recent disagreements, neither the IMF nor the U.S. Treasury Department has determined any country to be manipulating its exchange rate. There are differing views on why. Some argue that countries have not engaged in policies that violate international commitments on exchange rates or triggered provisions in U.S. law relating to currency manipulation. Others argue that currency manipulation has occurred, but that estimating a currency's "true" or "fundamental" value is complicated, and that the current international financial architecture is not effective at responding to exchange rate disputes.

Chapter 2 - China's policy of intervening in currency markets to limit or halt the appreciation of its currency, the renminbi (RMB), against the U.S. dollar and other currencies has been an issue of concern for many in Congress over the past decade who view it as one of several distortive economic and trade policies that are used to convey an unfair competitive advantage to Chinese producers and exporters. They charge that China's currency policy is intended to make its exports significantly less expensive, and its imports more expensive, than would occur if the RMB were a freely- traded currency. They argue that the RMB is significantly undervalued against the dollar and that this has been a major contributor to the large annual U.S. trade deficits with China and a significant decline in U.S. manufacturing jobs in recent years.

China began to peg the RMB to the dollar in 1994 at about 8.28 yuan (the base unit of the RMB) per dollar and kept the rate constant through July 2005, when, under pressure from its major trading partners, it moved to a managed peg system and began to allow the RMB to gradually appreciate over the next three years. In July 2008, China halted RMB appreciation because of the effects of the global economic crisis on China's exporters. It resumed RMB appreciation in June 2010. From July 2005 through June 2013, the RMB appreciated by 34% on a nominal basis against the dollar and by 42% on a real (inflation-adjusted) basis. Over the past few years, China's current account surplus has declined, and its accumulation of foreign exchange reserves has slowed—factors that have led some analysts to contend the RMB is not as undervalued against the dollar as it once was.

The effects of China's currency policy on the U.S. economy are complex. If the RMB is undervalued (as some contend), then it might be viewed as an indirect export subsidy which artificially lowers the prices of Chinese products imported into the United States. Under this view, this benefits U.S. consumers and U.S. firms that use Chinese-made parts and components, but could negatively affect certain U.S. import-competing firms and their workers. An undervalued RMB might also have the effect of limiting the level of U.S. exports to China than might occur under a floating exchange rate system. The United States is also affected by China's large purchases of U.S. Treasury securities. China's intervention in currency markets causes it to accumulate large levels of foreign exchange reserves, especially U.S. dollars, which it then uses to purchase U.S. debt. Such purchases help the U.S. government fund its budget deficits and help keep U.S. interest rates low. These factors suggest that an appreciation of the RMB to the dollar benefits some U.S. economic sectors, but negatively affects others.

The effects of the recent global financial crisis have refocused attention on the need to reduce global imbalances in savings, investment, and trade, especially with regard to China and the United States, in order to avoid future crises. Many economists contend that China should take greater steps to rebalance its economy by lessening its dependence on exports and fixed investment as the main drivers of its economic growth, while boosting the level of domestic consumer demand (which would increase Chinese imports).

A market-based currency policy is seen as an important factor in achieving this goal.

Currency bills aimed at addressing China's currency policy have been introduced in every session of Congress since 2003. The House approved a currency bill in the 111th Congress and the Senate passed one in the 112th Congress. Currency legislation has been proposed in the 113th Congress, including H.R. 1276 and S. 1114. In recent years, congressional concerns about undervalued currencies have moved beyond China to include those of several other countries as well.

Chapter 3 - A trend depreciation of the dollar since 2002 raises concern among some in Congress and the public that the dollar's decline is a symptom of broader economic problems, such as a weak economic recovery, rising public debt, and a diminished standing in the global economy. However, a falling currency is not always a problem, but possibly an element of economic adjustments that are, on balance, beneficial to the economy.

A depreciating currency could affect several aspects of U.S. economic performance. Possible effects include increased net exports, decreased international purchasing power, rising commodity prices, and upward pressure on interest rates; if the trend is sustained, the United states may also experience a reduction of external debt, possible undermining of the dollar's reserve currency status, and an elevated risk of a dollar crisis.

The exchange rate is not a variable that is easily addressed by changes in legislative policy. Nevertheless, although usually not the primary target, the dollar's international value can be affected by decisions made on policy issues facing the 112th Congress, including decisions related to generating jobs, raising the debt limit, reducing the budget deficit, and stabilizing the growth of the federal government's long-term debt. Also monetary policy actions by the Federal Reserve, over which Congress has oversight responsibilities, can affect the dollar.

The exchange rate of the dollar is largely determined by the market—the supply and demand for dollars in global foreign exchange markets associated with the buying and selling of dollar denominated goods, services, and assets (e.g., stocks, bonds, real property) on global markets. In most circumstances, however, international asset-market transactions will tend to be dominant, with the size and strength of inflows and outflows of capital ultimately determining whether the exchange rate appreciates or depreciates.

A variety of factors can influence the size and direction of cross-border asset flows. Of principal importance are the likely rate of return on the asset, investor expectations about a currency's future path, the size and liquidity of the country's asset markets, the need for currency diversification in international investors' portfolios, changes in the official holdings of foreign exchange reserves by central banks, and the need for and location of investment safe havens. All of these factors could themselves be influenced by economic policy choices.

To give Congress the economic context in which to view the dollar's recent and prospective movement, this report analyzes the evolution of the exchange rate since its peak in 2002. It examines several factors that are likely to influence the dollar's medium-term path, what effects a depreciating dollar could have on the economy, and how alternative policy measures that could be taken by the Federal Reserve, the Treasury, and the 112th Congress might influence the dollar's path.

Chapter 4 - Congress has been concerned, for many years, with the possible impact that currency manipulation has on international trade. The International Monetary Fund (IMF) has jurisdiction for exchange rate questions. The World Trade Organization (WTO) is responsible for the rules governing international trade. The two organizations approach the issue of "currency manipulation" differently. The IMF Articles of Agreement prohibit countries from manipulating their currency for the purpose of gaining unfair trade advantage, but the IMF cannot force a country to change its exchange rate policies. The WTO has rules against subsidies, but these are very narrow and specific and do not seem to encompass currency manipulation. Recently, some have argued that an earlier ruling by a WTO dispute resolution panel might be a way that currency issues could be included in the WTO prohibition against export subsidies. Congress is currently considering legislation to amend U.S. countervailing duty law, based on this precedent, that the proponents believe is consistent with WTO rules. Others disagree as to whether the previous case is a sufficient precedent.

Several options might be considered for addressing this matter in the future, if policymakers deem this a wise course of action. The Articles of Agreement of the IMF or the WTO Agreements could be amended in order to make their treatment of currency manipulation more consistent. Negotiations might be pursued, on a multilateral as well as a bilateral basis, to resolve currency manipulation disputes on a country-by-country basis without changing the IMF or WTO treatment of this concern. Some countries might argue that the actions of another violate WTO rules and seek a favorable decision by a WTO dispute resolution panel. Finally, the IMF and WTO could use their interagency agreement to promote better coordination in their treatment of this concern.

In: Exchange Rates and Currency Debates
Editor: Darren Byers

ISBN: 978-1-62948-616-1
© 2013 Nova Science Publishers, Inc.

Chapter 1

CURRENT DEBATES OVER EXCHANGE RATES: OVERVIEW AND ISSUES FOR CONGRESS[*]

Rebecca M. Nelson

SUMMARY

Exchange rates are important in the international economy, because they affect the price of every country's imports and exports, as well as the value of every overseas investment. Following the global financial crisis of 2008-2009 and ensuing economic recession, disagreements among countries over exchange rates have become more widespread. Some policy leaders and analysts contend that there is a "currency war" now underway among certain countries.

At the heart of current disagreements is whether or not countries are using exchange rate policies to undermine free markets and intentionally push down the value of their currency in order to gain a trade advantage at the expense of other countries. A weak currency makes exports cheaper to foreigners, which can lead to higher exports and job creation in the export sector. However, if one country weakens its currency, there can be implications for other countries. In general, exporters and firms producing import-sensitive goods may find it harder to compete against countries with weak currencies. However, consumers and businesses that

---

[*] This is an edited, reformatted and augmented version of a Congressional Research Service publication, CRS Report for Congress R43242, dated September 26, 2013.

rely on inputs from abroad may benefit when other countries have weak currencies, because imports may become cheaper.

The United States has found itself on both sides of the current debates over exchange rates. On one hand, some Members of Congress and U.S. policy experts argue that U.S. exports and U.S. jobs have been adversely affected by the exchange rate policies adopted by China, Japan, and a number of other countries. On the other hand, some emerging markets, including Brazil and Russia, have argued that expansionary monetary policies in the United States and other developed countries caused the currencies of developed countries to depreciate, hurting the competitiveness of emerging markets. More recently, however, emerging-market currencies have started to depreciate, and now there are concerns about emerging-market currencies becoming too weak relative to the currencies of some developed economies.

Through the International Monetary Fund (IMF), countries have committed to avoid "currency manipulation." There are also provisions in U.S. law to address "currency manipulation" by other countries. In the context of recent disagreements, neither the IMF nor the U.S. Treasury Department has determined any country to be manipulating its exchange rate. There are differing views on why. Some argue that countries have not engaged in policies that violate international commitments on exchange rates or triggered provisions in U.S. law relating to currency manipulation. Others argue that currency manipulation has occurred, but that estimating a currency's "true" or "fundamental" value is complicated, and that the current international financial architecture is not effective at responding to exchange rate disputes.

Policy Options for Congress

Some Members of Congress may consider addressing exchange rate issues because they are concerned about the impact of other countries' exchange rate policies on the competitiveness of U.S. products. Recently, concerns have been raised about the impact of Japan's economic policies on the value of the yen, and the implications for the U.S. economy. However, there are a number of potential consequences from taking action on exchange rates that Congress might also want to consider. For example, U.S. imports from countries with weak currencies may be less expensive than they would be otherwise; countries may retaliate after being labeled a currency "manipulator;" and tensions over exchange rates could dissipate as the global economy strengthens.

If Members did decide to take action, they have a number of options for doing so. Options could include urging the Administration to address currency disputes at the IMF and in trade agreements, or passing legislation relating to countries determined to have undervalued exchange rates, among others. Two bills have been introduced in the 113th Congress related to exchange rate policies in other countries (H.R. 1276; S. 1114). Congressman Levin has also released a proposal for addressing currency issues in the Trans-Pacific Partnership, a proposed free trade agreement that the United States is negotiating with Japan and 10 other Asia-Pacific countries.

INTRODUCTION

Some policymakers and analysts allege that certain countries are using exchange rate policies to gain an "unfair" trade advantage. They maintain that some countries are purposefully using various policies to weaken the value of their currency to boost exports and create jobs, but that these policies come at the expense of other countries. Some political leaders and policy experts contend that there is a "currency war" in the global economy, as countries compete against each other to weaken the value of their currencies and boost exports.[1]

The United States has found itself on both sides of the debate. On one hand, some Members of Congress and U.S. policy experts argue that U.S. producers and U.S. jobs have been adversely affected by the exchange rate policies adopted by China, Japan, and a number of other countries. On the other hand, some emerging markets, including Brazil and Russia, have argued that expansionary monetary policies in the United States and other major developed countries have reduced the value of the dollar and other currencies, and thereby have hurt the competitiveness of emerging markets. More recently, some in the United States have started discussing pulling back expansionary monetary policies, and emerging-market currencies have started to weaken. There are now concerns about emerging-market currencies becoming too weak relative to the currencies of some developed economies.

During the 113th Congress, some Members of Congress have proposed taking action on exchange rate issues:

- Legislation has been introduced aimed at countries determined to have fundamentally undervalued or misaligned exchange rates (the Currency Reform for Fair Trade Act, H.R. 1276; the Currency Exchange Rate Oversight Reform Act of 2013, S. 1114).

- Some Members have expressed concerns about Japan's monetary policies and its effect on exchange rates, which impact the competitiveness of U.S. exports. These concerns have been raised particularly in the context of the Trans-Pacific Partnership (TPP) negotiations. TPP is a proposed regional trade agreement that the United States is negotiating with Japan and 10 other countries in the Asia- Pacific region.[2] In June 2013, 230 Representatives sent a letter to President Obama urging the Administration to address unfair exchange rate policies in the TPP, particularly with regards to Japan.[3] In September 2013, 60 Senators sent a letter to the Treasury Secretary, Jacob Lew, and the U.S. Trade Representative, Michael Froman, asking them to address currency "manipulation" in the TPP and all future free trade agreements.[4] Congressman Levin released a specific proposal to address unfair exchange rate practices in the TPP in July 2013.[5]
- Some Members have also called on the Administration to address currency issues in negotiations with the European Union (EU) over a proposed free trade agreement (the Transatlantic Trade and Investment Partnership [TTIP]) and in renewal of Trade Promotion Authority (TPA).[6] TPA is the authority Congress grants to the President to enter into certain reciprocal trade agreements and to have their implementing bills considered under expedited legislative procedures when certain conditions have been met.[7] TPA expired in 2007 and some Members are looking to renew it to facilitate trade negotiations.

This report provides information on current debates over exchange rates in the global economy. It offers an overview of how exchange rates work; analyzes specific disagreements and debates; and examines existing frameworks for potentially addressing currency disputes. It also lays out some policy options available to Congress, should Members want to take action on exchange rate issues.

THE IMPORTANCE OF EXCHANGE RATES IN THE GLOBAL ECONOMY

What Is an Exchange Rate?

An exchange rate is the price of a country's currency relative to other currencies. In other words, it is the rate at which one currency can be converted into another currency. For example, on August 30, 2013, one U.S. dollar could be exchanged for 0.76 euros (€), 98 Japanese yen (¥), or 0.65 British pounds (£).[8] Exchange rates are expressed in terms of dollars per foreign currency, or expressed in terms of foreign currency per dollar. The exchange rate between dollars and euros on August 30, 2013 can be quoted as 1.32 $/€ or, equivalently, 0.76 €/$.

Consumers use exchange rates to calculate the cost of goods produced in other countries. For example, U.S. consumers use exchange rates to calculate how much a bottle of French or Australian wine costs in U.S. dollars. Likewise, French and Australian consumers use exchange rates to calculate how much a bottle of U.S. wine costs in euros or Australian dollars.

DIFFERENT MEASURES OF EXCHANGE RATES

- **Nominal vs. real exchange rate:** The nominal exchange rate is the rate at which two currencies can be exchanged, or how much one currency is worth in terms of another currency. The real exchange rate measures the value of a country's goods against those of another country at the prevailing nominal exchange rate. Essentially, the real exchange rate adjusts the nominal exchange rate for differences in prices (and rates of inflation) across countries.

- **Bilateral vs. effective exchange rate:** The bilateral exchange rate is the value of one currency in terms of another currency. The effective exchange rate is the value of a currency against a weighted average of several currencies (a "basket" of foreign currencies). The basket can be weighted in different ways, such as by share of world trade or GDP. The Bank for International Settlements (BIS), for example, publishes data on effective exchange rates.[10]

How much a currency is worth in relation to another currency is determined by the supply and demand for currencies in the foreign exchange market (the market in which foreign currencies are traded). The foreign exchange market is substantial, and has expanded in recent years. Trading in foreign exchange markets averaged $5.3 trillion per day in April 2013, up from $3.3 trillion in April 2007.[9]

The relative demand for currencies reflects the underlying demand for goods and assets denominated in that currency, and large international capital flows can have a strong influence on the demand for various currencies. The government, typically the central bank, can use policies to shape the supply of its currency in international capital markets.

Impact on International Trade and Investment

International Trade

Exchange rates affect the price of every export leaving a country and every import entering a country. As a result, changes in the exchange rate can impact trade flows. When the value of a country's currency falls, or depreciates, relative to another currency, its exports become less expensive to foreigners and imports from overseas become more expensive to domestic consumers.[11] These changes in relative prices can cause the level of exports to rise and the level of imports to fall.[12] For example, if the dollar depreciates against the British pound, U.S. exports become cheaper to UK consumers, and imports from the UK become more expensive to U.S. consumers. As a result, U.S. exports to the UK may rise, and U.S. imports from the UK may fall.

Likewise, when the value of a currency rises, or appreciates, the country's exports become more expensive to foreigners and imports become less expensive to domestic consumers. This can cause exports to fall and imports to rise. For example, if the dollar appreciates against the Australian dollar, U.S. exports become more expensive to Australian consumers, and imports from Australia become less expensive to U.S. consumers. Changes in prices may cause U.S. exports to Australia to fall and U.S. imports from Australia to rise.

International Investment

Exchange rates impact international investment in two ways. First, exchange rates determine the value of existing overseas investments. When a currency depreciates, the value of investments denominated in that currency falls for overseas investors. Likewise, when a currency appreciates, the value of investments denominated in that currency rises for overseas investors. For example, if a U.S. investor holds a German government bond denominated in euros, and the euro depreciates, the value of the bond in U.S. dollars falls, making the investment worth less to the U.S. investor. In contrast, if the euro appreciates, the value of the German bond in U.S. dollars rises, and the investment is worth more to the U.S. investor.

Second, exchange rates impact the flow of investment across borders. Changes in the value of a currency today can shape investors' future expectations about the value of the currency, which can have substantial impacts on capital flows. If investors expect a currency to depreciate, overseas investors may be reluctant to invest in assets denominated in that currency and may want to sell assets denominated in the currency, in fear that their investments will become less valuable over time. Likewise, if a currency is expected to rise over time, assets denominated in that currency become more attractive to overseas investors. For example, a depreciating euro may deter U.S. investment in the Eurozone, while an appreciating euro may increase U.S. investment in the Eurozone. [13]

Types of Exchange Rate Policies

There are two major ways that the price of a country's currency is determined, or types of "currency regimes." First, some governments "float" their currencies. This means they allow the price of its currency to fluctuate depending on supply and demand for currencies in foreign exchange markets. Governments with floating exchange rates do not take policy actions to influence the value of their currencies.

Second, some countries "fix" or "peg" their exchange rate. This means they fix the value of their currency to another currency (such as the U.S. dollar or euro), a group (or "basket") of currencies, or a commodity, such as gold. The government (typically the central bank) then uses various policies to control the supply and demand for the currency in foreign exchange markets to maintain the set price for the currency. Often, central banks maintain exchange rate pegs by buying and selling currency in foreign exchange markets, or "intervening" in foreign exchange markets.

There are pros and cons to having a floating or fixed exchange rate. Fixed exchange rates provide more certainty in international transactions, but they can make it more difficult for the economy to adjust to economic shocks and can make the currency more susceptible to speculative attacks. Floating exchange rates introduce more unpredictability in international transactions and may deter international trade and investment, but make it easier for the economy to adjust to changes in economic conditions.

In order to take advantage of the benefits of both fixed and floating exchange rates, many countries do not adopt a purely fixed or floating exchange rate, but choose a hybrid policy: they let the currency's value fluctuate but take action to keep the exchange rate from deviating too far from a target value or zone. The degree to which they float or peg varies. The optimal choice for any given country will depend on its characteristics, including its size and interconnectedness to the country to which it would peg its currency.

Between the end of World War II and the early 1970s, most countries, including the United States, had fixed exchange rates.[14] In the early 1970s, when international capital flows increased, the United States abandoned its peg to gold and floated the dollar. Other countries' currencies were pegged to the dollar, and after the dollar floated, some other countries decided to float their currencies as well.

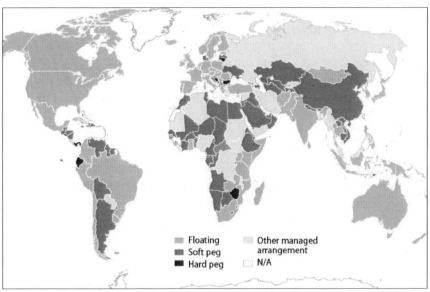

Source: IMF, "Annual Report on Exchange Arrangements and Exchange Restrictions," 2012.
Notes: See footnote 15.

Figure 1. Map of Exchange Rate Policies by Country.

In 2012, 35% of countries had floating currencies.[15] This includes several major currencies, such as the U.S. dollar, the euro, the Japanese yen, and the British pound, whose economies together account for 50% of global GDP.[16] Many countries use policies to manage the value of their currencies, although some manage it more than others. This includes many small countries, such as Panama and Hong Kong, as well as a few larger economies, such as China, Russia, and Saudi Arabia. In 2012, 40% of countries used a "soft" peg, which let the exchange rate fluctuate within a desired range, and 13% of countries used a "hard" peg, which anchors the currency's value more strictly, including the formal adoption of a foreign currency to use as a domestic currency (for example, Ecuador has adopted the U.S. dollar as its national currency).[17] No large country uses a hard peg. **Figure 1** depicts the exchange rate policies adopted by different countries.

Exchange Rate Misalignments

Many economists believe that exchange rate levels can differ from the underlying "fundamental" or "equilibrium" value of the exchange rate. When an actual exchange rate differs from its fundamental or equilibrium value, the currency is said to be misaligned. More specifically, when the actual exchange rate is too high, the currency is said to be overvalued; when the actual rate is too low, the currency is said to be undervalued.

Considerable debate exists about what the fundamental or equilibrium value of a currency is and how to define or calculate currency misalignment.[18] For example, some economists believe that a currency is misaligned when the exchange rate set by the government, or the official rate, differs from what would be set by the market if the currency were allowed to float. By this reasoning, governments that take policy actions to sustain an exchange rate peg, such as intervening in currency markets, most likely have misaligned currencies. Additionally, this view suggests that floating currencies, by definition, cannot be misaligned, since their values are determined by market forces.

For other economists, a currency can be misaligned even if it is a floating rate. This is the case if the exchange rate differs from its long-term equilibrium value, which is based on economic fundamentals and eliminates short-term factors that can cause the exchange rate to fluctuate. Defining or estimating an equilibrium exchange rate is not a straightforward process and is complex. Economists disagree on the factors that determine an equilibrium exchange rate, and whether the concept is a valid one, particularly when applied to countries with floating exchange rates. Economists have developed a number of models for calculating differences between actual exchange rates and equilibrium exchange rates. Estimates of whether a currency is misaligned, and if so, by how much, can vary widely depending on the model used.[19]

GENERAL DEBATES OVER "CURRENCY WARS"

Amid heightened concerns about slow growth and high unemployment in many countries, disagreements over exchange rate policies have broadened after the global financial crisis. In 2010, Brazil's finance minister, Guido Mantega, declared that a "currency war" had broken out in the global economy.[20]

At the heart of current disagreements is whether or not countries are using policies to intentionally push down the value of their currency in order to gain a trade advantage at the expense of other countries. A weak currency makes exports cheaper to foreigners and imports more expensive to domestic consumers. This can lead to higher production of exports and import-competing goods, which could help spur export-led growth and job creation in the export sector.

However, if one country weakens its currency, there can be negative implications for certain sectors in other countries. In general, a weaker currency in one country can hurt exporters in other countries, since their exports become relatively more expensive and may fall as a result. Additionally, domestic firms producing import-competing goods may find it harder to compete with imports from countries with weak currencies, since weak currencies lower the cost of imports. Under certain circumstances, policies used to drive down the value of a currency in one country can cause other countries to run persistent trade deficits (imports exceed exports) that can be difficult to adjust and can be associated with the build-up of debt.

For these reasons, some economists view efforts to boost exports through a weaker exchange rate as "unfair" to other countries and a type of "beggar-thy-neighbor" policy—the benefit the country gets from the policy comes at the expense of other countries. These views are particularly rooted in the experience in the 1930s, during which, some economists argue, countries devalued their currencies to boost exports, in response to widespread high unemployment and negative economic conditions.[21] The devaluations in the 1930s are referred to as "competitive devaluations," since a devaluation in one country was often offset by a devaluation in another country, making it difficult for any country to gain a lasting advantage.[22] Some economists view the competitive devaluations of the 1930s as detrimental to international trade, and, in addition to protectionist trade policies, as exacerbating the Great Depression.

Many economists disagree that "currency wars" and competitive devaluations are currently underway in the global economy, and if they are, that they are not necessarily bad for the global economy. Because currency devaluations can often involve printing domestic currency, or implementing expansionary monetary policies, they can stimulate short-term economic growth.[23] If enough countries engage in currency interventions, then there may be no net change in relative exchange rate levels and the simultaneous currency interventions may help reflate the global economy and boost global economic growth. Economists of this viewpoint argue that competitive devaluations of the 1930s did not cause the Great Depression and, in fact, actually helped end it.[24]

Additionally, a weak currency in one country does not have an unambiguous negative effect on other countries. Instead, consumers and certain sectors may benefit when other countries have weak currencies. In particular, consumers that purchase imports from abroad benefit when other countries have weak currencies, because imports become cheaper. Additionally, businesses that rely on inputs from overseas also benefit when other countries have weak currencies, by lowering the costs of inputs and thus the overall cost of production.

SPECIFIC DEBATES OVER EXCHANGE RATES

In current debates about exchange rates and whether countries are engaged in unfair currency policies to weaken their currencies, two major types of concerns have been raised: first, concerns about countries engaged in interventions in foreign currency markets, and second, concerns about the effects of expansionary monetary policies in some developed countries on exchange rate levels.

Currency Interventions

Governments have various mechanisms they can use to weaken, or devalue, their currency, or sustain a lower exchange rate than would exist in the absence of government intervention. One way is intervening in foreign exchange markets or, more specifically, selling domestic currency in exchange for foreign currency. These interventions increase the supply of domestic currency relative to other currencies in foreign exchange markets, pushing the price of the currency down. The foreign currency is typically then invested in foreign assets, most commonly government bonds.

Concerns about currency interventions are not new. For nearly a decade, various policymakers and analysts have raised concerns about China's interventions in foreign exchange markets to maintain, in their view, an undervalued currency relative to the U.S. dollar. Since the global financial crisis, however, concerns about currency interventions have become more widespread, as more countries, including Switzerland and others, have intervened in foreign exchange markets, in the view of some analysts, to lower the value of their currency.[25]

China[26]

Over the past decade, the Chinese government has tightly managed the value of its currency, the renminbi (RMB) or yuan, against the U.S. dollar.[27] Some policymakers and analysts believe that China's currency policies keep the RMB undervalued relative to the U.S. dollar. They argue that China's policies give Chinese exports an "unfair" trade advantage against U.S. exports and are a major contributing factor to the U.S. trade deficit with China.

In 1994, China began to peg its currency to the U.S. dollar and kept it pegged to the U.S. dollar at a constant rate through 2005. In July 2005, it moved to a managed peg system, in which the government allowed the currency to fluctuate within a range, and the currency began to appreciate. In 2008, China halted appreciation of the RMB, due to concerns about the effects of the global financial crisis on Chinese exports. In 2012, China again allowed more flexibility in the value of the RMB against the U.S. dollar. Between 2005 and the end of 2012, the RMB appreciated by almost 25% against the dollar (**Figure 2**).[28]

The Chinese government has used various policies, including intervening in foreign currency markets and capital controls, to manage this appreciation of the RMB against the U.S. dollar. It does so primarily by printing yuan and selling it for U.S. currency and assets denominated in U.S. dollars, usually

U.S. government bonds. It also manages the value of its exchange rate through capital controls that limit buying and selling of RMB.[29] As China has engaged in currency interventions, its holdings of foreign exchange reserves has increased, from $715 billion in the first quarter of 2005 to $3,463 billion in the first quarter of 2013 (**Figure 2**), equivalent to about 38% of China's GDP.[30] Some economists view the sustained, substantial increase in foreign exchange reserves as evidence that the Chinese government keeps the value of the RMB below what it would be if the RMB were allowed to float freely.

More recently, some economists are starting to question whether the yuan is still undervalued against the U.S. dollar when adjusting for differences in price levels (the real exchange rate), and if so, by how much, particularly as inflation has increased in China.[31] They point to the fact that foreign exchange reserves have not grown as quickly since 2011 as some evidence of this adjustment. In July 2012, the IMF changed its assessment of the RMB's value from significantly undervalued to moderately undervalued.[32]

Switzerland

Before the global financial crisis of 2008-2009, Switzerland had a floating exchange rate. During the crisis, the Swiss franc was viewed as a "safe haven" currency, or a currency that investors trusted more than others and would therefore buy in times of uncertainty.[33] Increased investor demand for the Swiss franc put upward pressure on the currency, which, in turn, raised concerns for the Swiss government about the competitiveness of Swiss exports. In 2009 and 2010, the Swiss central bank (the National Bank of Switzerland) intervened in foreign exchange markets to prevent or limit appreciation of the Swiss franc against the euro, by selling Swiss francs for foreign currencies.[34] When a worsening of the Eurozone crisis put additional upward pressure on the Swiss franc, the Swiss central bank announced in September 2011 that it would buy "unlimited quantities" of foreign currency to keep the Swiss franc from appreciating above a specific value (**Figure 3**).[35] As a result of its currency interventions, Switzerland's foreign exchange reserves increased more than tenfold, from $46 billion in the fourth quarter of 2008 to $470 billion in the first quarter of 2013 (**Figure 3**), about 73% of Swiss GDP.[36] Before the financial crisis, the Swiss central bank had last intervened in the foreign exchange market in 1995.[37]

Many economists argue that the recent interventions by the Swiss central bank have held the value of the Swiss franc lower than it would be otherwise (if the currency floated freely and the Swiss central bank did not intervene in foreign exchange markets). They argue that this has given Swiss exports an advantage, helping Switzerland maintain a trade surplus and one of the lowest unemployment rates in Europe.[38] However, some economists have noted that Switzerland's trading partners have generally not "kicked up much fuss" over its interventions, and that Switzerland's interventions are the "overlooked" currency war in Europe.[39] This could be due to the small size of the Swiss economy, and a perception held by some that Swiss interventions are a defensive measure against developments in the rest of Europe that are beyond its control.

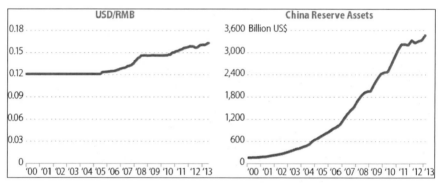

Source: Federal Reserve; IMF, International Financial Statistics.
Note: For the graph on the left, an increase represents an appreciation of the RMB relative to the U.S. dollar.

Figure 2. China's Exchange Rate and Foreign Exchange Reserves.

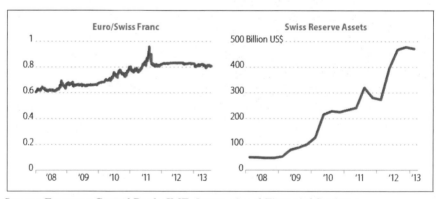

Source: European Central Bank; IMF, International Financial Statistics.
Note: For the graph on the left, an increase represents an appreciation of the Swiss franc relative to the euro.

Figure 3. Switzerland's Exchange Rate and Foreign Exchange Reserves.

Other Countries

Other examples of interventions to weaken currencies since the global financial crisis include, among others:

- **Japan**, which sold yen in foreign exchange markets in 2010 and 2011. Japan's interventions in March 2011 were unusual in that they were supported with corresponding interventions by the other G-7 countries to weaken the yen. A crisis in Japan (earthquake, tsunami, and threat of nuclear crisis) in March 2011 had sparked a sharp appreciation of the yen, which some feared would throw the world's third largest economy back into recession, prompting the coordinated interventions;[40]
- **South Korea**, which is believed to have intervened in currency markets intermittently to hold down the value of the won in the latter part of 2012 and early 2013;[41] and
- **New Zealand**, whose central bank revealed in May 2013 that it had intervened in currency markets to stem appreciation of its currency, the New Zealand dollar (nicknamed the kiwi).[42]

More generally, according to a December 2012 study by the Peterson Institute of International Economics (PIIE), more than 20 countries have cumulatively increased their foreign exchange reserves by nearly $1 trillion annually for several years, mainly through interventions in foreign currency markets, and as a result have been able to keep their currencies "substantially undervalued."[43] The study identifies China, Denmark, Hong Kong, South Korea, Malaysia, Singapore, Switzerland, and Taiwan as most heavily engaged in currency interventions.

Debates

A number of countries are actively intervening, or have recently intervened, in foreign exchange markets to lower the value of their currencies, and there are different views among economists about the consequences of these interventions for other countries. Some economists argue that currency interventions have helped countries give their exports a boost at the expense of other countries. The December 2012 study by the PIIE estimates that currency interventions have caused the U.S. trade deficit to increase by $200 billion to $500 billion per year and the U.S. economy to lose between one million and five million jobs.[44] The study also argues that currency interventions have adversely affected the economies of Australia, Brazil, Canada, the Eurozone, India, and Mexico, in addition to a number of other developing economies.

Other economists are skeptical that one country's interventions in foreign exchange markets have had adverse consequences for other countries. For example, some economists argue that interventions in foreign exchange markets by other countries changes the composition of output in the United States (particularly the size of the export and domestic-oriented sectors), but does not reduce the overall employment or output levels in the U.S. economy. Some economists also question whether currency interventions have long-lasting effects on exchange rate levels, particularly for countries with floating currencies. They argue that the large size of international capital flows overwhelm, in the long-term, government purchases and sales of foreign currencies, and that other economic fundamentals, such as interest rates, inflation rates, and overall economic performance, have much greater effects on exchange rate levels.

Still other economists argue that it is hard to make generalizations about the effects of currency interventions, and that, depending on the specific circumstances, currency interventions may or may not be "fair" policies.[45] For example, they argue that relevant factors can include:

- **Does the government intervene in currency markets to sometimes strengthen and sometimes weaken its currency, or does it always intervene to weaken its currency?** "Two-way" interventions (sometimes strengthening the currency, sometimes weakening the currency) may be evidence that the country is using currency interventions to sustain a pegged exchange rate that is close to its long- term fundamental or equilibrium value. Some economists argue that "one-way" interventions (always selling domestic currency) may be evidence that the government is using interventions to sustain a currency that is below the currency's fundamental or equilibrium value.
- **Does the government intervene periodically, or on a continual basis?** Periodic interventions may smooth potentially disruptive short-term fluctuations in the exchange rate and help the country build foreign exchange reserves, which can help it guard against economic crises. Sustained, or long-term, interventions may create negative distortions in the global economy.
- **Does the government allow the intervention to increase its domestic money supply, or does the government "sterilize" the**

Current Debates Over Exchange Rates

intervention to prevent an increase in its domestic money supply? When some governments intervene in currency markets by selling domestic currency, they allow the domestic money supply to increase. This is called an unsterilized intervention. When other countries (such as China and, sometimes, Switzerland) intervene, they do not allow their money supply to increase. Instead, when they sell domestic currency in exchange for foreign currency, they then sell a corresponding quantity of domestic government bonds to remove the extra domestic currency from circulation. This is called a sterilized intervention. It may matter to other countries whether the intervening country sterilizes the intervention or not. For example, increasing the money supply may help increase domestic demand, which in certain circumstances can cause consumers to buy more, not fewer, imports from other countries. Additionally, an increase in the money supply may cause prices to rise in the medium-term. This may mean that the exchange rate adjusted for inflation (the real exchange rate) may not change in the medium- term (after prices adjust), even if the nominal exchange rate (the exchange rate not adjusted for inflation) falls.

Expansionary Monetary Policies

In addition to intervening directly in foreign exchange markets, governments can weaken the value of their currency through expansionary monetary policies. Monetary policy is the process by which a government (usually the central bank) controls the supply of money in an economy, such as by changing the interest rates through buying and selling government bonds. Changes in the money supply can impact the value of the currency. For example, increasing the supply of British pounds can cause the price of the pound to fall.

Some emerging markets, particularly Brazil, have been critical of the expansionary monetary policies adopted by the United States, the United Kingdom, and the Eurozone in response to the global financial crisis of 2008-2009. A number of countries have also raised concerns about Japan's monetary policies, following a major policy shift in late 2012 and early 2013.

Quantitative Easing in the United States, UK, and Eurozone[46]
The United States, the United Kingdom, and, to a lesser extent, the Eurozone adopted expansionary monetary policies to respond to the economic

recession following the global financial crisis of 2008-2009. In addition to cutting interest rates, the Federal Reserve, the Bank of England, and the European Central Bank (ECB) used quantitative easing to provide further monetary stimulus. Quantitative easing is an unconventional form of monetary policy that expands the money supply through government purchases of assets, usually government bonds. Quantitative easing is typically used when more conventional monetary policy tools are no longer feasible, for example, when short-term interest rates cannot be cut because they are already near zero.

Some emerging markets have argued that because the U.S. dollar, the British pound, and the euro are floating currencies, expansionary policies in these countries have caused these currencies to depreciate against the currencies of emerging markets. For example, Brazil has argued that quantitative easing in developed countries was a key factor in causing its currency (the real) to appreciate by more than 25% against the dollar between the start of 2009 and the end of the third quarter of 2010 (see **Figure 4**), when Brazil's finance minister, Guido Mantega, declared that a currency "war" had broken out in the global economy.[47] Brazil imposed some short-term controls on inflows of capital into Brazil (capital controls) to stem appreciation of the real.[48]

In response to the concerns of emerging markets, many policymakers and analysts have argued that the Federal Reserve, the Bank of England, and the ECB adopted expansionary monetary policies for domestic purposes (combatting the recession), and that any effect on their currencies was a side-effect or by-product of the policy.[49] For example, during a Senate Banking Committee hearing in February 2013, the Chairman of the Federal Reserve, Ben Bernanke, stressed that the Federal Reserve is not engaged in a currency war or targeting the value of the U.S. dollar.[50]

Instead, he emphasized that monetary policy is being used to achieve domestic economic objectives (high employment and price stability). He also stressed that monetary policies to strengthen aggregate demand in the United States are not "zero-sum," because they raise the demand for the exports of other countries.

The concerns of emerging markets about the effects of quantitative easing have eased in recent months. As developed countries have started discussing rolling back expansionary monetary policies, the real has weakened substantially against the U.S. dollar (see **Figure 4**). Brazil's government, in fact, has started expressing concerns about the real becoming too weak, and in

August 2013, intervened in foreign currency markets to strengthen its currency.[51] The concerns of emerging-market economies about the potential rollback of quantitative easing policies in developed countries, including the United States, was a major topic of discussion at the September 2013 G-20 summit in St. Petersburg, Russia.[52]

Japan and "Abenomics"

Concerns have also been recently raised about major changes in Japan's monetary policy and their effects on the value of the yen. Elected in December 2012, Prime Minister Shnizo Abe has made it a priority of his administration to grow Japan's economy and eliminate deflation (falling prices), which has plagued Japan for many years. His economic plan, nicknamed "Abenomics," relies on three major economic policies: expansionary monetary policies, fiscal stimulus, and structural reforms. To promote expansionary monetary policy, Japan's central bank (the Bank of Japan) unveiled a host of new measures in the first half of 2013, including goals to double the monetary base (commercial bank reserves plus currency circulating in the public) and to double its holdings of Japanese government bonds. By buying government bonds in exchange for yen, the Bank of Japan can increase Japan's money supply.

Changes in Japan's monetary policies, along with fiscal stimulus measures, appear to be contributing to a strengthening of Japan's economy. For example, in July 2013, the IMF upgraded its forecast of growth in Japan for 2013, from 1.5% to 2.0%.[53] However, the expansionary monetary policies may have also contributed to a relatively sharp depreciation of the yen, which fell more than 25% between mid-2012 and mid-2013 (see **Figure 5**), even as Japan has not directly intervened in currency markets since 2011.

Several countries have expressed their concerns about a weakenin g of the yen. An official from the Russian central bank reportedly warned that "Japan is weakening the yen and other countries may follow," and that "the world is on the brink of a fresh currency war."[54] Additionally, the president of China's sovereign wealth fund reportedly warned Japan against using its neighbors as a "garbage bin" by deliberately devaluing the yen, and South Korea's finance minister argued that Japan's weakening yen hurts his country's economy more than threats from North Korea.[55] Movements in Japan's currency have also created concerns for some Members of Congress, with concerns being raised about the currency policies in the context of the TPP, where Japan is one of the negotiating parties.

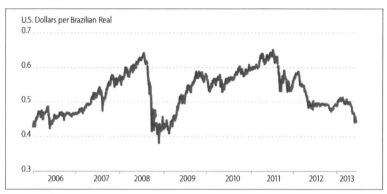

Source: Federal Reserve.
Note: An increase represents an appreciation of the Brazilian real relative to the U.S. dollar.

Figure 4. U.S. Dollar-Brazilian Real Exchange Rate.

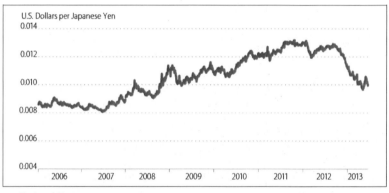

Source: Federal Reserve.
Note: A decrease represents a depreciation of the yen relative to the U.S. dollar.

Figure 5. U.S. Dollar-Japanese Yen Exchange Rate.

Others argue that a weakening yen in recent months has partially offset the slow, but continued, appreciation of the yen in the preceding several years (**Figure 5**). For example, in January 2012, the IMF estimated that the Japanese yen was "moderately overvalued from a medium-term perspective."[56] Some also argue that, rather than targeting the value of the currency, Japan's monetary policies are targeting domestic objectives, namely, beating deflation that has plagued the economy for many years. Japan's finance minister, Taro Aso, reportedly stated that "monetary easing is aimed at pulling Japan out of deflation quickly. It is not accurate at all to criticize (us) for manipulating currencies."[57]

Debates

There is debate over whether the expansionary monetary policies, including quantitative easing, implemented by some developed economies have been "beggar-thy-neighbor" policies. Some argue that expansionary monetary policies have unfairly caused the currencies of developed countries to depreciate against other countries, giving the exports of developed countries an "unfair" export boost. However, most economists agree that the expansionary policies in the United States, the UK, the Eurozone, and Japan have been designed to stimulate their domestic economies and will, in the medium-term, cause prices to rise. As a result, they argue that there will be little effect on the real exchange rate (the exchange rate adjusted for differences in prices across countries) in the medium-term (as prices increase), even if the nominal exchange rate (the exchange rate not adjusted for differences in prices across countries) falls in the short-term. However, it should be noted that inflation in all these countries remains very low, to date.

Additionally, some argue that the expansionary policies stimulate domestic consumption and investment, which ordinarily leads to higher, not lower, imports from other countries, all else being equal.[58] They argue that the net effect of quantitative easing and similar policies on trading partners is not necessarily negative and could be positive in some instances. For example, the IMF estimated that the first round of quantitative easing in the United States resulted in substantial output gains for the rest of the world, and that the second round generated modest output gains for the rest of the world.[59]

For some economists, then, a key question to evaluate whether expansionary monetary policies are "fair" or "unfair" in the context of claims about "currency wars" is:

- **Is it appropriate for countries to adopt expansionary monetary policies to combat a domestic economic recession, even if some sectors in other countries may be adversely affected in the short-run?:** Some economists argue that it is entirely "natural" for countries to unilaterally adopt the monetary policies to suit their specific needs of the domestic economy, and that countries should use expansionary monetary policies to respond to economic recessions.[60] Moreover, most central banks, including the Fed, are pursuing statutory mandates that do not include foreign exchange rate requirements and responsibilities. Other economists argue that countries have a number of policy tools to respond to economic recessions, not just monetary policy, and that in today's globalized economy, a country should consider the potential negative spillover effects on other countries in its decision-making process.

ADDRESSING DISAGREEMENTS OVER EXCHANGE RATES

Government policies that impact exchange rates have been a source of contention among countries. Various avenues have been developed or explored over the years to address specific currency disputes, both at the multilateral level and through U.S. law, with varying degrees of impact.

On the multilateral front, countries have made commitments to refrain from "manipulating" their exchange rates to gain an unfair trade advantage through the International Monetary Fund (IMF). Additionally, some argue that commitments made in the context of the World Trade Organization (WTO) are relevant to disagreements over exchange rates, although this view is disputed. Exchange rate issues have also been addressed in the past through less formal channels of international economic coordination among small groups of developed economies.

In addition to these multilateral forums, the United States has also adopted legislation to address unfair exchange rate policies pursued by other countries. In 1988, Congress enacted legislation to address "currency manipulation" by other countries. Congress has also included provisions on exchange rates in previous TPA legislation.

Exchange rate issues have been a key source of discussion at recent G-7 and G-20 meetings, but little formal or concrete action has occurred beyond these discussions.[61] Neither the IMF nor the U.S. Treasury Department has found any country to be manipulating its exchange rate in recent years.

Forums to Potentially Address Disagreements

International Monetary Fund

With a nearly universal membership of 188 countries, the IMF is focused on promoting international monetary stability.[62] The IMF has engaged on the exchange rate policies of its member countries as part of its mandate, arguably motivated by the experience of competitive devaluations in the 1930s.[63] Its role on exchange rates has evolved over time.[64] Currently, IMF member countries have agreed to several obligations on exchange rates in the IMF's Articles of Agreement, the document that lays out the rules governing the IMF and establishes a "code of conduct" for IMF member countries.[65] The Articles state that countries can use whatever exchange rate system they wish—fixed or floating—so long as they follow certain guidelines; that countries should seek, in their foreign exchange and monetary policies, to promote orderly economic growth and financial stability; and that the IMF should engage in "firm" surveillance over the exchange rate policies of its members.[66]

The Articles also state that IMF member countries are to "avoid manipulating exchange rates or the international monetary system in order to prevent effective balance of payments adjustment or to gain an unfair advantage over other members."[67] An IMF Decision, issued in 1977 and updated in 2007 and 2012, provides further guidance that, among other things, "a member will only be considered to be manipulating exchange rates in order to gain an unfair competitive advantage over other members if the Fund determines both that: (a) the member is engaged in these policies for the purposes of securing fundamental exchange rate misalignment in the form of an undervalued exchange rate; and (b) the purpose of securing such misalignment is to increase net exports."[68]

If a member country were to be found to be in violation of its obligations to the IMF, under the rules laid out in the Articles, it could be punished through restrictions on its access to IMF funding, suspension of its voting rights at the IMF, or, ultimately, expulsion from the IMF.[69]

To date, the IMF has never publicly labeled a member country a currency manipulator.[70] Some argue that the IMF's definition of currency "manipulation" has made it tough to go after currency "manipulators." They argue that it requires the IMF to determine or demonstrate that policies shaping the exchange rate level have been for the express purpose of increasing net exports, and that "intent" is hard to establish.[71] Even if the IMF could demonstrate a country is manipulating its exchange rate under its definition of the term, some analysts also argue that, in practice, the IMF does not have a credible mechanism for dealing with "manipulators," particularly countries that are not reliant on IMF financing.[72] They argue that it is extremely unlikely the IMF would actually strip violators of their IMF voting rights or expel them from the institution.

World Trade Organization

With 159 member countries, the WTO is the principal international organization governing world trade. It was established in 1995 as a successor institution to the General Agreement on Tariffs and Trade (GATT), a post-World War II institution intended to liberalize and promote nondiscrimination in trade among countries. Unique among the major international trade and finance organizations, the WTO has a mechanism for enforcing its rules through a dispute settlement process.

Given the relationship between exchange rates and trade, some have argued that the World Trade Organization (WTO) has a role to play in responding to currency disputes. Some analysts and lawyers have examined whether WTO provisions allow for recourse against countries that are unfairly undervaluing its currency.[73]

One aspect of the debate is whether WTO agreement on export subsidies applies to countries with undervalued currencies. The WTO Agreement on Subsidies and Countervailing Measures specifies that countries may not provide subsidies to help promote their national exports, and countries are entitled to levy countervailing duties on imported products that receive subsidies from their national government.[74] Some economists maintain that an undervalued currency lowers a firm's cost of production relative to world prices and therefore helps encourage exports. Some argue, then, that an undervalued currency should count as an export subsidy. It is not clear, however, whether intentional undervaluation of a country's currency is an export subsidy under the WTO's specific definition of the term, and thus is eligible for recourse through countervailing duties under WTO agreements. For example, the subsidy must be, among other things, specific to an industry and not provided generally to all producers. There is debate over whether intentional undervaluation of a currency is "industry specific" because it applies to everyone.

Another aspect of the debate relates to a provision in the GATT (the WTO agreement on international trade in goods), which states that member countries "shall not, by exchange action, frustrate intent of the provisions" of the agreement.[75] Some analysts argue that policies to undervalue a currency are protectionist policies, and thus should count as an exchange rate action that frustrates the intent of the GATT. Others argue that the language is too vague to apply to undervalued currencies.[76] Specifically, they argue that the language was written to apply to an international system of exchange rates that no longer exists (the system of fixed exchange rates, combined with capital controls, that prevailed from the end of World War II to the early 1970s).

No dispute over exchange rates has been brought before the WTO,[77] and whether currency disputes fall under the WTO's jurisdiction remains a contested issue.[78]

Less Formal Multilateral Coordination: The G-7 and the G-20

In addition to formal international institutions focused on economic issues, like the IMF and the WTO, countries also use less formal forums to coordinate economic policies. Before the global financial crisis of 2008-2009, the primary forum was a small group of seven advanced economies, the G-7.[79] Following the crisis, the G-20, a larger group of advanced and emerging-market countries became the premier forum for international economic coordination.[80]

In the past, small groups of advanced economies had had more success in addressing currency issues through this type of less formal international cooperation. For example, in 1985, France, West Germany, Japan, the United States, and the UK signed the Plaza Accord, in which countries agreed to intervene in currency markets to depreciate the U.S. dollar in relation to the Japanese yen and the German deutsche mark to address the U.S. trade deficit. In 1987, six countries (the five signatories of the Plaza Accord, plus Canada) signed the Louvre Accord, in which they agreed to halt the depreciation of the U.S. dollar through a host of different policy measures, including taxes, public spending, and interest rates. Some economists argue that the Plaza and Louvre Accords were successful because they reinforced economic fundamentals that were pushing exchange rates in the desired direction.

Additionally, small groups of countries have executed coordinated interventions in foreign exchange markets to shape the relative value of currencies. For example, the G-7 countries have coordinated interventions a number of times: in 1995, to halt the dollar's fall against the yen; in 2000, to support the value of the euro after its introduction; and in 2011, to stem appreciation of the yen following a major crisis in Japan.[81] This coordination has occurred on an ad hoc, voluntary basis. It is not based on any specific set of rules or commitments on exchange rates, and has been limited to a small group of advanced economies.

U.S. Law: The 1988 Trade Act

In 1988, Congress enacted the "Exchange Rates and International Economic Policy Coordination Act of 1988" as part of the Omnibus Trade and Competitiveness Act of 1988 (the 1988 Trade Act),[82] when many policymakers were concerned about the appreciation of the U.S. dollar and large U.S. trade deficits.[83] A key component of this Act requires the Treasury

Department to analyze on an annual basis the exchange rate policies of foreign countries, in consultation with the IMF, and "consider whether countries manipulate the rate of exchange between their currency and the United States dollar for purposes of preventing effective balance of payments adjustments or gaining unfair competitive advantage in international trade." If "manipulation" is occurring with respect to countries that have (1) global currency account surpluses and (2) significant bilateral trade surpluses with the United States, the Secretary of the Treasury is to initiate negotiations, through the IMF or bilaterally, to ensure adjustment in the exchange rate and eliminate the "unfair" trade advantage. The Secretary of the Treasury is not required to start negotiations in cases where they would have a serious detrimental impact on vital U.S. economic and security interests.

Additionally, the Act requires the Treasury Secretary to submit a report annually to the Senate and House Banking Committees, on or before October 15, with written six-month updates (on April 15), and is expected to testify on the reports as requested.[84] The reports are to address a host of issues related to exchange rate policies, such as: currency market developments; currency interventions undertaken to adjust the exchange rate of the dollar; the impact of the exchange rate on U.S. competitiveness; and the outcomes of Treasury negotiations on currency issues, among others.

Since the 1988 Trade Act was enacted, the Treasury Department has identified three countries as manipulating their currencies under the Trade Act's terms: China, Taiwan, and South Korea.[85]

These designations occurred in the late 1980s and early 1990s; Treasury has not found currency manipulation under the terms of the 1988 Trade Act since it last cited China in 1994. Some Members of Congress have been concerned by what they perceive as inaction by the Treasury Department on currency manipulation. In 2004, Congress passed legislation asking the Treasury Secretary to submit a report "describing how statutory provisions addressing currency manipulation by America's trading partners... can be better clarified administratively to provide for improved and more predictable evaluation, and to enable the problem of currency manipulation to be better understood by the American people."[86] In 2005, the Government Accountability Office (GAO) completed a study on Treasury's assessments of whether countries manipulate their currencies for trade advantage.[87] One conclusion in the report was that, "Treasury has generally complied with the reporting requirements for its exchange rate reports, although its discussion of U.S. economic impacts has become less specific over time."

Trade Promotion Authority and Trade Agreements

Given the potential links between exchange rate policies of other countries and the competitiveness of U.S. industry and exports, Congress has referenced addressing currency issues in previous TPA authorizations. For example, in the Omnibus Trade and Competitiveness Act of 1988, which granted "fast track" authority (the precursor to TPA) to the President, the President was required, among other things, to submit a report to Congress with supporting information after entering a trade agreement. One part of this report was "describing the efforts made by the President to obtain international exchange rate equilibrium."[88]

Additionally, when TPA was last renewed in 2002, Congress included exchange rate issues as a priority that the Administration should promote. The legislation stipulated that the Administration should "seek to establish consultative mechanisms among parties to trade agreements to examine the trade consequences of significant and unanticipated currency movements and to scrutinize whether a foreign government engaged in a pattern of manipulating its currency to promote a competitive advantage in international trade."[89]

A number of free trade agreements (FTAs) were negotiated under the 2002 version of TPA, with Congress approving implementing legislation for FTAs with Chile, Singapore, Australia, Morocco, the Dominican Republic and the Central American countries (CAFTA-DR), Bahrain, Oman, Peru, Colombia, Panama, and South Korea. It is not clear to what extent currency issues were salient issues in the negotiations or in the final agreements.

Responses to Current Disagreements

To the extent that there has been a formal multilateral response to current disagreements over exchange rates, it has been through discussions at G-7 and G-20 meetings. During meetings in February 2013, for example, the G-7 nations reaffirmed their "long-standing commitment to market-determined exchange rates" and to "not target exchange rates." [90] The G-20 countries pledged to "refrain from competitive devaluation" in February 2013,[91] and more recently in September 2013, that central banks "have committed that future changes to monetary policy settings will continue to be carefully calibrated and clearly communicated."[92] G-7 and G-20 commitments are non-binding, although other enforcement mechanisms, including peer pressure, have been used to ensure compliance in the past.

Current disagreements over exchange rates have not resulted in the IMF or the Treasury Department labeling any countries as currency manipulators, and no country has filed a dispute over exchange rate policies at the WTO. Starting in 2011, Brazil did present three papers on exchange rates and the role of the WTO for discussion at the WTO Working Group on Trade, Debt, and Finance. Reportedly, many other WTO members have approached the discussions with "reserve and skepticism" and believed that the IMF would be the appropriate forum for such a discussion.[93]

Some analysts and policymakers have been concerned that current disagreements have not resulted in more formal action, particularly by the IMF and the Treasury Department, which have the clearest rules pertaining to currency manipulation. They argue that currency manipulation has occurred, but the current frameworks are ineffective at dealing with it. For example, they argue that it is hard to demonstrate that exchange rate policies have been for the express purpose of increasing net exports; the IMF does not have a clear enforcement mechanism for its rules on exchange rates; and the Treasury Department fears retaliation from countries it unilaterally labels as "manipulators." One policy expert has stated that the greatest flaw in the international financial architecture is its failure to effectively counter and deter competitive currency policies.[94]

Other analysts and policymakers contend that the current frameworks on "currency manipulation" are effective. They argue that formal action by the IMF and the Treasury Department has not occurred because countries have not engaged in policies that violate international commitments on exchange rates or triggered U.S. laws pertaining to currency manipulation. Some analysts also believe that the Treasury Department has at various times urged countries to address exchange rate issues behind-the-scenes, even if it has not publicly labeled any countries as currency manipulators in recent years.[95]

POLICY OPTIONS FOR CONGRESS

Some Members of Congress have proposed taking action on currency issues, because they are concerned about the impact of other countries' exchange rate policies on the competitiveness of U.S. exports and import-competing firms. Some Members could also be concerned that other countries have accused the United States of engaging in "currency wars." If Members did decide to take action on exchange rates, there are a number of options for

Current Debates Over Exchange Rates 29

doing so, some of which Members are already pursuing. Policy options could include, among others:

(1) Maintaining the status quo: Even though Members may be concerned about supporting U.S. exports and jobs from "unfair" exchange rate policies adopted by other countries, there may be a number of reasons to refrain from taking action on exchange rate disputes:

- There is much debate among economists on how to calculate a currency's "equilibrium" or "fundamental" long-term value, making the classification of currencies as undervalued or overvalued complex and subject to much discussion, with different models at times yielding very different results. Some economists also believe that currency interventions have limited, short-term effects, particularly on floating currencies, given the high volumes of capital flows.

- U.S. imports from trading partners with weak currencies are less expensive than they would be otherwise. Lower-cost imports may benefit U.S. businesses that purchase inputs from abroad and U.S. consumers.

- Unilaterally labeling a country as a currency manipulator or leading a multilateral charge against currency manipulation could trigger retaliation by other countries. For example, the United States has a low savings rate and benefits from low interest rates. Countries labeled as currency "manipulators" could buy fewer U.S. government bonds, making it more expensive and potentially harder for the U.S. government to finance its budget deficit.

- Tensions over exchange rates could dissipate as the global economy strengthens, particularly if developed economies end quantitative easing. For example, Brazil's concerns about the real appreciating against the U.S. dollar have reversed in recent months (and now Brazil is concerned about the real depreciating against the U.S. dollar too much).

(2) Urging the Administration to address currency disputes at the IMF or WTO: Addressing currency disputes in formal international institutions may provide broad, multilateral support for decisions that are reached. The IMF and the WTO have been the international institutions identified as best suited for dealing with exchange rate disputes, because the IMF has the clearest set of commitments relating to currency manipulation, and the WTO is unique among international financial institutions that it has a clear enforcement mechanism. However, addressing disputes over exchange rates at the IMF and WTO may run into obstacles. For example, the IMF Executive Board may find it too politically sensitive to label a country as a "currency manipulator." Congress could ask the Administration to push for changes to IMF and/or WTO rules to allow currency disputes to be addressed more clearly under these organizations, but this could be a complicated process that requires multilateral consensus.

(3) **Urging the Administration to strengthen informal international cooperation on exchange rates:** For example, Congress could urge the Treasury Department to continue its push for G-20 commitments on: (1) greater transparency of foreign reserve data and currency intervention operations; and (2) avoidance of official public statements intended to influence exchange rate levels.[96] Additionally, Congress could also urge the Administration to push for informal agreements to re-align the value of currencies, similar to the Plaza Accord and the Louvre Accord in the 1980s. However, some question whether informal cooperation can effectively foster cooperation on exchange rates consistently, not just on an as-needed or ad-hoc basis. The G-7 excludes large emerging market economies that are major players in the global economy, but, at the same time, the G-20 may be too large and heterogeneous to reach meaningful agreements. Also, since agreements reached at the G-7 and G-20 are non-binding, questions have been raised about the effectiveness of these forums. This approach would also be unlikely to address manipulation by countries outside the G-7 or G-20, although some argue that G-20 action in particular would involve the major economies in the international economy.

(4) **Addressing currency issues in trade agreements or as a negotiating objective in TPA:** Congress could address concerns about the exchange rate policies of other countries by urging the Administration to address currency issues in the free trade agreements currently under negotiation, including the TPP and TTIP. For example, Congressman Levin released a proposal to address currency manipulation in the TPP in July 2013.[97] With regards to any legislation renewing TPA, Congress could also identify currency issues as a trade policy priority, similar to the provisions included in

the 2002 TPA legislation, or include currency issues as a more formal trade negotiating objective.

Seeking to include currency issues in a trade agreement could make the agreement more difficult to conclude. There are also different views about how currency issues could or should be addressed. Some have called for enforceable provisions, but there may be disagreement over how exchange rate disputes would be adjudicated. Others have called for cooperative frameworks to examine currency issues. Additionally, any negotiated agreement on currency disagreements would be limited in scope, because it would apply to negotiating parties to the agreement and not to countries in the global economy more broadly.

(5) **Passing new legislation on undervalued exchange rates or amending existing legislation on currency manipulation:** Some argue that legislation could directly address the concerns of certain U.S. exporters and import-sensitive producers about "unfair" exchange rate policies of other countries, and could provide U.S. exporters with recourse and/or encourage other countries to push up the value of their currencies. Additionally, a possible advantage of legislation relating to countries with "undervalued" or "misaligned" currencies is that it could apply to all countries, not just a subset of countries, such as countries that are party to a trade negotiation with the United States

Several pieces of legislation on exchange rates have been introduced in previous Congresses, and two bills have been introduced in the 113th Congress:

- **The Currency Reform for Fair Trade Act (H.R. 1276)** would affect the treatment of imports from countries with fundamentally undervalued exchange rates. If passed, it would broaden the definition of a "countervailable" subsidy (or a subsidy that could be eligible to be offset through higher import duties) to include the benefit conferred on merchandise imports into the United States from foreign countries with fundamentally undervalued currencies.[98]

- **The Currency Exchange Rate Oversight Reform Act of 2013 (S. 1114)** proposes methods for addressing exchange rate issues. Among other provisions, the legislation prescribes negotiations and consultations with countries with fundamentally misaligned exchange rates, and actions to take against "priority action" countries that have failed, or persistently failed, to take action to eliminate exchange rate misalignments.[99]

Others argue that it could be difficult to reach consensus on if, and if so, by how much, a currency is undervalued or misaligned. Additionally, if currency "manipulation" was defined in statute, it could be inflexible. As mentioned earlier, unilateral legislation could also provoke countries that are labeled as having undervalued currencies, and cause them to retaliate in ways that undermine other U.S. interests. Legislation could also harm U.S. producers and consumers that buy and use imported goods. Finally, some have raised questions about whether legislation relating to import duties would violate WTO rules.

CONCLUSION

Exchange rates are important prices in the global economy, and changes in exchange rates have potentially substantial implications for international trade and investment flows across countries. Following the global financial crisis of 2008-2009, tensions among countries over exchange rate policies have arguably broadened. Some policymakers and analysts have expressed concerns that some governments are pursuing exchange rate policies to gain a trade advantage, as many countries grapple with economic recession or slow growth and high unemployment following the financial crisis. Concerns have focused on both government interventions in currency markets in a number of other countries, including China and Switzerland, and expansionary monetary policies in some developed economies. On the other hand, some economists argue that the effects of exchange rate policies are nuanced, creating winners and losers, and that it is hard to make generalized claims about the negative effects of "currency wars."

Members concerned about the competitiveness of the United States may want to weigh the pros and cons of taking action on exchange rate disputes. If policymakers do want to take action, a number of policy options are available. Some Members of Congress have proposed legislation to address currency undervaluation by other countries and proposed addressing currency issues in on-going trade negotiations, particularly in the context of the proposed TPP and any renewal of TPA. Members could also urge the Administration to press the issue more forcefully at international institutions, such as the IMF or

Current Debates Over Exchange Rates

WTO, or more informal forums for international cooperation, including the G-7 or the G-20.

To date, the most formal response to current tensions over exchange rates has been through discussions at G-7 and G-20 meetings. Although frameworks have been set up for addressing currency "manipulation" at the IMF and through U.S. law, neither the IMF nor the U.S. Treasury Department has taken formal action on current disputes over exchange rates. There are debates about why formal action has not been taken at these institutions. One general complicating factor in addressing currency disputes is that estimating a currency's "fundamental" or "true" value is extremely complex and subject to debate among economists.

End Notes

[1] For example, see "Brazil Warns of World Currency War," *Reuters*, September 28, 2010; Fred Bergsten, "Currency Wars, the Economy of the United States, and Reform of the International Monetary System," Remarks at Peterson Institute for International Economics, May 16, 2013, http://www.iie.com/publications/papers/bergsten201305.pdf.

[2] For more information on TPP, see CRS Report R42694, *The Trans-Pacific Partnership Negotiations and Issues for Congress*, coordinated by Ian F. Fergusson.

[3] Congressman Mike Michaud, "Majority of House Members Push Obama to Address Currency Manipulation in TPP," Press Release, June 6, 2013, http://michaud.house.gov/press-release/majority-house-members-push-obama-address- currency-manipulation-tpp.

[4] Senator Debbie Stabenow, "Sixty Senators Urge Administration to Crack Down on Currency Manipulation in Trans- Pacific Partnership Talks," Press Release, September 24, 2013, http://www.stabenow.senate.gov/?p=press_release&id=1171.

[5] U.S. Representative Sander Levin, "U.S.-Japan Automotive Trade: Proposal to Level the Playing Field," http://www.piie.com/publications/papers/levin20130723proposal.pdf.

[6] For example, see U.S. Congress, House Ways and Means, *U.S. Trade Representative Michael Froman*, 113th Cong., 1st sess., July 18, 2013; U.S. Congress, Senate Finance, *Confirmation Hearing on the Nomination of Michael Froman to be U.S. Trade Representative*, 113th Cong., 1st sess., June 6, 2013. For more on TTIP, see CRS Report R43158, *Proposed Transatlantic Trade and Investment Partnership (TTIP): In Brief*, by Shayerah Ilias Akhtar and Vivian C. Jones. For more information about TPA, see CRS Report RL33743, *Trade Promotion Authority (TPA) and the Role of Congress in Trade Policy*, by J. F. Hornbeck and William H. Cooper.

[7] For more on TPA, see CRS Report RL33743, *Trade Promotion Authority (TPA) and the Role of Congress in Trade Policy*, by J. F. Hornbeck and William H. Cooper.

[8] Exchange rate data in this report is from the Federal Reserve, unless otherwise noted.

[9] Bank for International Settlements, "Foreign Exchange Turnover in April 2013: Preliminary Global Results," Triennial Central Bank Survey, September 2013, https://www.bis.org/publ/rpfx13fx.pdf.

[10] For example, see "BIS Effective Exchange Rate Indices," http://www.bis.org/statistics/eer/.

[11] This assumes that changes in the exchange rate are reflected in retail and consumer prices. In practice, there may be factors that limit the "pass through" of changes in the exchange rates

34 Rebecca M. Nelson

to changes in prices. For example, contracts may lock in prices of imports and exports for a set amount of time.

[12] It may take time for changes in the exchange rate to result in changes in the volume of tradable goods and services. For example, if imports become more expensive, it may take time for domestic consumers to find suitable domestic or foreign substitutes.

[13] The Eurozone refers to the 17 European Union (EU) member states that use the euro as their currency: Austria, Belgium, Cyprus, Estonia, Finland, France, Germany, Greece, Ireland, Italy, Luxembourg, Malta, the Netherlands, Portugal, Slovakia, Spain, and Slovenia. The other 10 EU members have yet to adopt the euro or have chosen not to adopt the euro.

[14] Exchange rates were, in theory, fixed but "adjustable," meaning that countries could adjust their exchange rates to correct a "fundamental disequilibrium" in their exchange rate. In practice, it was rare for a country to adjust its exchange rate outside of a narrow band.

[15] IMF, "Annual Report on Exchange Arrangements and Exchange Restrictions," 2012, http://www.imf.org/external/pubs/nft/2012/eaer/ar2012.pdf. Exchange rate data on how the exchange rate policies work in practice (the "*de facto*" exchange rate policy), which may or may not match the official description of the policy (the "*de jure*" exchange rate policy). Countries that are members of a currency union (where multiple countries may adopt use of the same currency, including the Eurozone, the East Caribbean Currency Union, the West African Economic and Monetary Union, and the Central African Economic Community) are coded according to how the currency is managed. For example, the euro is a floating currency, and individual members of the Eurozone for this purpose are counted as having adopted floating exchange rates.

[16] IMF, *World Economic Outlook Database*, April 2013.

[17] 13% use other managed arrangements that do not fall neatly into a "soft" peg or "hard" peg category, sometimes because the government changes exchange rate policies frequently.

[18] For example, see Enzo Cassino and David Oxley, "Exchange Rate Valuation and its Impact on the Real Economy," New Zealand Treasury, March 2013, http://www.rbnz.govt.nz/research_and_publications/seminars_and_workshops/mar2013/5200821.pdf; Rebecca L. Driver and Peter F. Westaway, " Concepts of Equilibrium Exchange Rates," Bank of England, Working Paper No. 248, 2004, http://www.bankofengland.co.uk/publications/Documents/workingpapers/wp248.pdf.

[19] For example, see "Misleading Misalignments," *Economist*, June 21, 2007; Peter Isard, "Equilibrium Exchange Rates: Assessment Methodologies," IMF Working Paper WP/07/296, December 2007, http://www.imf.org/external/pubs/ft/wp/2007/wp07296.pdf; Treasury Department, "Semiannual Report on International Economic and Exchange Rate Policies," December 2006, Appendix 2, Exchange Rate Misalignment: What the Models Tell Us and Methodological Considerations," http://www.treasury.gov/resource-center/international/exchange-rate- policies/Documents/2006_Appendix-2.pdf.

[20] For example, see "Brazil Warns of World Currency War," *Reuters*, September 28, 2010.

[21] For example, see Beth A. Simmons, *Who Adjusts? Domestic Sources of Foreign Economic Policy During the Interwar Years.* (Princeton, NJ: Princeton University Press, 1994). Not all economists characterize changes in exchange rates during the 1930s as competitive devaluations. For example, some argue that countries were forced to devalue because they were running out of gold reserves. See Douglas A. Irwin, *Trade Policy Disaster: Lessons from the 1930s* (Cambridge, MA: MIT Press, 2012).

[22] Depreciation is typically used to refer to a currency weakening due to market forces. When a government undertakes specific policies to weaken the value of its currency, it is typically referred to as a devaluation.

[23] For example, see Matthew O'Brien, "Currency Wars, What Are They Good For? Absolutely Ending Depressions," *The Atlantic*, February 5, 2013.

[24] Barry Eichengreen, "Currency War or International Policy Coordination?," University of California, Berkeley, January 2013, http://emlab.berkeley.edu/~eichengr/curr_war_JPM_2013.pdf.

Current Debates Over Exchange Rates

[25] For example, see Alan Beattie, "Hostilities Escalate to Hidden Currency War," *Financial Times*, September 27, 2010.

[26] For more on China's currency, see CRS Report RL32165, *China's Currency: Economic Issues and Options for U.S. Trade Policy*, by Wayne M. Morrison and Marc Labonte.

[27] The official name of China's currency is the renminbi (RMB), which is denominated in yuan units. Both RMB and yuan are used interchangeably to refer to China's currency.

[28] Change in the nominal exchange rate (not adjusted for differences in inflation between China and the United States).

[29] The RMB is largely convertible on a current account (trade) basis, but not on a capital account basis, meaning that foreign exchange in China is not regularly obtainable for investment purposes. In other words, it can be difficult to purchase investments denominated in RMB.

[30] IMF, *International Financial Statistics*, 2013; IMF, *World Economic Outlook*, April 2013.

[31] "The Cheapest Thing Going is Gone," *Economist*, June 15, 2013.

[32] IMF, "IMF Executive Board Concludes 2012 Article IV Consultation with People's Republic of China," Public Information Notice No. 12/86, July 24, 2012, http://www.imf.org/external/np/sec/pn/2012/pn1286.htm; Simon Rabinovitch, "IMF Says Renminbi 'Moderately Undervalued'," *Financial Times*, July 25, 2012.

[33] Michael Bordo, Owen F. Humpage, Anna J. Schwartz, "Foreign-Exchange Intervention and the Fundamental Trilemma of International Finance: Notes for Currency Wars," *VoxEU*, June 18, 2012, http://www.voxeu.org/article/notes-currency-wars-trilemma-international-finance.

[34] U.S. Department of the Treasury, Office of International Affairs, "Report to Congress on International Economic and Exchange Rate Policies," July 8, 2010, http://www.treasury.gov/resource-center/international/exchange-rate-policies/Documents/Foreign%20Exchange%20Report%20July%202010.pdf.

[35] Swiss National Bank Press Release, September 6, 2011, http://www.snb.ch/en/mmr/reference/pre_20110906/source/pre_20110906.en.pdf.

[36] IMF, *International Financial Statistics*, 2013; IMF, *World Economic Outlook*, April 2013.

[37] Michael Bordo, Owen F. Humpage, Anna J. Schwartz, "Foreign-Exchange Intervention and the Fundamental Trilemma of International Finance: Notes for Currency Wars," *VoxEU*, June 18, 2012, http://www.voxeu.org/article/notes-currency-wars-trilemma-international-finance.

[38] Daniel Gros, "An Overlooked Currency War in Europe," *VoxEU*, October 11, 2012, http://www.voxeu.org/article/overlooked-currency-war-europe.

[39] Ibid., "Positive-Sum Currency Wars," *Economist*, February 14, 2013.

[40] Peter Garnham and David Oakley, "G7 Nations Co-ordinate $25bn Yen Sell-Off," *Financial Times*, March 18, 2011.

[41] According to the April 2013 Treasury report on exchange rates, the Korean government does not publish intervention data, but many market participants believe that the Korean authorities intervened in currency markets in the latter part of 2012 and early 2013. See U.S. Department of the Treasury, Office of International Affairs, "Report to Congress on International Economic and Exchange Rate Policies," April 12, 2013, http://www.treasury.gov/resource-center/international/exchange-rate-policies/Documents/Foreign%20Exchange%20Report%20April%202013.pdf.

[42] Alan Beattie, "Hostilities Escalate to Hidden Currency War," *Financial Times*, September 27, 2010; U.S. Department of the Treasury, Office of International Affairs, "Report to Congress on International Economic and Exchange Rate Policies," April 12, 2013, http://www.treasury.gov/resource-center/international/exchange-rate-policies/Documents/Foreign%20Exchange%20Report%20April%202013.pdf; Rebecca Howard, "NZ Central Bank Admits Currency Intervention to Dampen Dollar," *Dow Jones*, May 9, 2013.

[43] C. Fred Bergsten and Joseph E. Gagnon, "Currency Manipulation, the US Economy, and the Global Economic Order," Peterson Institute for International Economics Policy Brief 12-25, December 2012, http://www.iie.com/publications/interstitial.cfm?ResearchID=2302.

[44] Ibid.

[45] For example, see Matthew O'Brien, "Currency Wars, What Are They Good For? Absolutely Ending Depressions," *The Atlantic*, February 5, 2013; "Trial of Strength," *Economist*, September 23, 2010.

[46] For more on quantitative easing in the United States, see CRS Report R42962, *Federal Reserve: Unconventional Monetary Policy Options*, by Marc Labonte.

[47] For example, see "Brazil Warns of World Currency War," *Reuters*, September 28, 2010. In this report, exchange rate data is from the Federal Reserve unless otherwise noted.

[48] Samantha Pearson, "Brazil Launches Fresh 'Currency War' Offensive," *Financial Times*, March 15, 2012.

[49] For example, see "Phoney Currency Wars," *Economist*, February 16, 2013.

[50] U.S. Congress, Senate Banking, Housing, and Urban Affairs, *Hearing on the Semi-Annual Monetary Policy Report*, 113th Cong., 1st sess., February 26, 2013.

[51] For example, see Matthew Malinowski and Blake Schmidt, "Brazil Real Surges on $60 Billion Intervention Plan," *Bloomberg*, August 23, 2013.

[52] G-20 Leaders' Declaration, September 2013, St. Petersburg, http://www.g20.org/documents.

[53] IMF, *World Economic Outlook Update*, July 9, 2013, http://www.imf.org/external/pubs/ft/weo/2013/update/02/.

[54] Simon Kennedy and Scott Rose, "Russia Says World is Nearing Currency War as Europe Joins," *Bloomberg*, January 16, 2013.

[55] Lingling Wei, "China Fund Warns Japan Against a 'Currency War,'" *Wall Street Journal*, March 6, 2013; Cynthia Kim, "South Korea's Hyun Says Yen Bigger Issue than North Korea," *Bloomberg*, April 18, 2013.

[56] IMF, "Japan: Solid Recovery, but Europe Dampens Outlook," IMF Survey Online, June 12, 2012, http://www.imf.org/external/pubs/ft/survey/so/2012/car061112b.htm.

[57] "Japan Denies Currency Manipulation Claims Ahead of G20," *Reuters*, January 25, 2013.

[58] "Positive-Sum Currency Wars," *Economist*, February 14, 2013.

[59] IMF, "The United States Spillover Report – 2011 Article IV Consultation," IMF Country Report No. 11/203, July 2011, pp. 32, http://www.imf.org/external/pubs/ft/scr/2011/cr11203.pdf.

[60] For example, see Jeffrey Frankel, "Dispatches from the Currency Wars," *Project Syndicate*, June 11, 2013. http://www.project-syndicate.org/blog/dispatches-from-the-currency-wars.

[61] The Group of 7 (G-7) includes Canada, France, Germany, Italy, Japan, the United States, and the United Kingdom. The Group of 20 (G-20) includes the G-7 countries plus Argentina, Australia, Brazil, Canada, China, India, Indonesia, Mexico, Russia, Saudi Arabia, South Africa, South Korea, Turkey, and the European Union (EU). For more on the G- 20, see CRS Report R40977, *The G-20 and International Economic Cooperation: Background and Implications for Congress*, by Rebecca M. Nelson.

[62] For more on the IMF, CRS Report R42019, *International Monetary Fund: Background and Issues for Congress*, by Martin A. Weiss.

[63] For example, see Morris Goldstein, "Currency Manipulation and Enforcing the Rules of the International Monetary System," in *Reforming the IMF for the 21st Century*, ed. Edwin M. Truman, Special Report 19 ed. (Institute for International Economics, 2006), http://www.piie.com/publications/chapters_preview/3870/05iie3870.pdf.

[64] Between the end of World War II and the early 1970s, the IMF supervised a fixed exchange rate system, in which the value of all currencies was fixed to the U.S. dollar, and the value of the dollar was fixed to gold. Countries could not change their exchange rates by more than 10% without the Fund's consent, and could only do so to correct a "fundamental disequilibrium" in exchange rate values. This system broke down in the early 1970s when the United States floated its currency, and some other countries subsequently decided to float their currencies as well. After a period of turmoil in world currency markets, an amendment to the IMF's founding document—the Articles of Agreement—was adopted in 1978. This Amendment laid out member countries' obligations on exchange rate policies to incorporate the shift to floating currencies adopted by some IMF member countries.

Current Debates Over Exchange Rates

[65] IMF Articles of Agreement (as amended), http://www.imf.org/External/Pubs/FT/AA/#art4.

[66] IMF Article IV.

[67] Effective balance of payments adjustment generally refers to a country's ability to, over time, balance its international transactions, particularly relating to the capital account (financial transactions) and its current account (export and import of goods and services, plus income and other unilateral transfers, such as gifts or remittances).

[68] IMF, "IMF Executive Board Adopts New Decision on Bilateral Surveillance over Members' Policies," Public Information Notice (PIN) No. 07/69, June 21, 2007, http://www.imf.org/external/np/sec/pn/2007/pn0769.htm; IMF, "IMF Executive Board Adopts New Decision on Bilateral and Multilateral Surveillance," Public Information Notice (PIN) No. 12/89, July 30, 2012, http://www.imf.org/external/np/sec/pn/2012/pn1289.htm.

[69] IMF Articles of Agreement, Article XXVI:2.

[70] Joseph E. Gagnon, "Combating Widespread Currency Manipulation," Peterson Institute for International Economics Policy Brief PB12-19, July 2012, http://www.iie.com/publications/pb/pb12-19.pdf.

[71] Claus D. Zimmermann, "Exchange Rate Misalignment and International Law," *The American Journal of International Law*, vol. 105, no. 3 (July 2011), pp. 423-476.

[72] Ibid.

[73] For example, see Robert W. Staiger and Alan O. Sykes, "'Currency Manipulation' and World Trade," *World Trade Review*, vol. 9, no. 4 (2010), pp. 583-627; Haneul Jung, "Tackling Currency Manipulation with International Law: Why and How Currency Manipulation Should be Adjudicated?," *Manchester Journal of International Economic Law*, vol. 9, no. 2 (2012), pp. 184-200.

[74] WTO Agreement on Subsidies and Countervailing Measures, http://www.wto.org/english/docs_e/legal_e/24- scm.pdf.

[75] GATT Article XV(4), http://www.wto.org/english/docs_e/legal_e/gatt47_01_e.htm#articleXV.

[76] For example, see Aaditya Mattoo and Arvind Subramanian, "Currency Undervaluation and Sovereign Wealth Funds: A New Role for the World Trade Organization," Peterson Institute for International Economics Working Paper WP 08- 2, January 2008, http://www.petersoninstitute.org/publications/wp/wp08-2.pdf; Gary Hufbauer, Yee Wong, and Ketki Sheth, *US-China Trade Disputes: Rising Tide, Rising Stakes*. Policy Analyses in International Economics 78. Washington: Institute for International Economics, 2006; Michael Waibel, "Retaliating Against Exchange-Rate Manipulation under WTO Rules," *VoxEU*, April 16, 2010, http://www.voxeu.org/article/retaliating-against-exchange-rate-manipulation-under-wto-rules.

[77] Robert E. Scott, "Currency Manipulation—History Shows that Sanctions are Needed," Economic Policy Institute, April 29, 2010, http://www.epi.org/publication/pm164/.

[78] Gregory Hudson, Pedro Bento de Faria, and Tobias Peyerl, "The Legality of Exchange Rate Undervaluation Under WTO Law," Geneva Graduate Institute, Center for Trade and Economic Integration Working Paper, July 2011, http://graduateinstitute.ch/webdav/site/ctei/shared/CTEI/working_papers/CTEI-2011-07.pdf.

[79] The Group of 7 (G-7) includes Canada, France, Germany, Italy, Japan, the United States, and the United Kingdom.

[80] The Group of 20 (G-20) includes the G-7 countries plus Argentina, Australia, Brazil, Canada, China, India, Indonesia, Mexico, Russia, Saudi Arabia, South Africa, South Korea, Turkey, and the European Union (EU). For more on the G-20, see CRS Report R40977, *The G-20 and International Economic Cooperation: Background and Implications for Congress*, by Rebecca M. Nelson.

[81] "Divine Intervention," *Economist*, March 27, 2008.

[82] P.L. 100-418; 22 U.S.C. 5301-5306.

[83] C. Randall Henning, "Congress, Treasury, and the Accountability of Exchange Rate Policy: How the 1988 Trade Act Should be Reformed," Institute for International Economics Working Paper 07-8, September 2007, http://www.iie.com/publications/wp/wp07-8.pdf.

[84] The Treasury Department also posts the currency reports on its website: http://www. treasury.gov/resource-center/international/exchange-rate-policies/Pages/ index.aspx.

[85] Treasury cited Taiwan and South Korea in 1988 and China in 1992. Taiwan's and South Korea's citations lasted for at least two 6-month reporting periods, while China's lasted for five 6-month reporting periods. Taiwan was cited again in 1992. U.S. Government Accountability Office, *Treasury Assessments Have Not Found Currency Manipulation, but Concerns about Exchange Rates Continue*, GAO-05-351, April 2005, http://www.gao.gov/ assets/250/246061.pdf.

[86] Section 221 of the Consolidated Appropriations Act, 2005 (P.L. 108-447).

[87] U.S. Government Accountability Office, *Treasury Assessments Have Not Found Currency Manipulation, but Concerns about Exchange Rates Continue*, GAO-05-351, April 2005, http://www.gao.gov/assets/250/246061.pdf. 88 Section 1103(a)(2)(B)(iii) of the Omnibus Trade and Competitiveness Act of 1988 (P.L. 100-418).

[89] Section 2102(c)(12) of the Trade Act of 2002 (P.L. 107-210).

[90] Bank of England; News Release – G7 Statement, February 12, 2013, http://www. bankofengland.co.uk/publications/Pages/news/2013/027.aspx.

[91] Charles Clover, Robin Harding, and Alice Ross, "G20 Agrees to Avoid Currency Wars," *Financial Times*, February 17, 2013; G-20 Communiqué, Meeting of Finance Ministers and Central Bank Governors, Moscow, February 15-16, 2013, available at http://www. g20.org/documents/.

[92] G-20 Leaders' Declaration, September 2013, St. Petersburg, http://www.g20.org/documents.

[93] Vera Thorstensen, Daniel Ramos, and Caronlina Muller, "The 'Missing Link' Between the WTO and IMF," *Journal of International Economic Law*, vol. 16, no. 2 (2013), pp. 353-381.

[94] Fred Bergsten, "Currency Wars, the Economy of the United States, and Reform of the International Monetary System," Remarks at Peterson Institute for International Economics, May 16, 2013, http://www.iie.com/publications/papers/bergsten201305.pdf.

[95] For example, see Annie Lowrey, "A Tightrope on China's Currency," *New York Times*, October 22, 2012.

[96] U.S. Department of the Treasury, Office of International Affairs, "Report to Congress on International Economic and Exchange Rate Policies," April 12, 2013, http://www.treasury. gov/resource-center/international/exchange-rate- policies/Documents/Foreign%20Exchange %20Report%20April%202013.pdf.

[97] U.S. Representative Sander Levin, "U.S.-Japan Automotive Trade: Proposal to Level the Playing Field," http://www.piie.com/publications/papers/levin20130723proposal.pdf. The proposal calls for, among other things, a commitment by TPP countries to avoid manipulating exchange rates to gain an unfair competitive advantage over other TPP countries; establishing specific benchmarks by which to determine whether a TPP country has manipulated its exchange rate; and enforcing commitments to avoid exchange rate manipulation through the normal dispute settlement mechanism of the TPP agreement.

[98] The bill provides details on how it would be determined if a country had a fundamentally undervalued currency, and the size of the real effective exchange rate undervaluation. Introduced by Congressman Levin, it is similar to bills introduced by Congressman Levin in the 112th Congress (H.R. 639) and in the 111th Congress (H.R. 2378). The House passed H.R. 2378 in September 2010.

[99] More generally, the bill requires the Treasury Department to issue a semiannual report to Congress on international monetary policy and exchange rates; prescribes negotiations and consultations with countries with fundamentally misaligned exchange rates, and actions to take against "priority action" countries that have failed, or persistently failed, to take action to eliminate the fundamental exchange rate misalignment; requires the Treasury Secretary to oppose any proposed changes in the international financial institutions that would increase the representation of countries with fundamentally misaligned currencies that are designated for priority action; amends countervailing and antidumping duty legislation to incorporate imports from countries with fundamentally misaligned currencies; and

establishes an Advisory Committee on International Exchange Rate Policy. It would also repeal the Exchange Rates and International Economic Policy Coordination Act of 1988. Introduced by Senator Brown, this bill is similar to S. 1619, which Senator Brown introduced in the 112th Congress and was passed by the Senate in October 2011.

In: Exchange Rates and Currency Debates
Editor: Darren Byers

ISBN: 978-1-62948-616-1
© 2013 Nova Science Publishers, Inc.

Chapter 2

CHINA'S CURRENCY POLICY: AN ANALYSIS OF THE ECONOMIC ISSUES[*]

Wayne M. Morrison and Marc Labonte

SUMMARY

China's policy of intervening in currency markets to limit or halt the appreciation of its currency, the renminbi (RMB), against the U.S. dollar and other currencies has been an issue of concern for many in Congress over the past decade who view it as one of several distortive economic and trade policies that are used to convey an unfair competitive advantage to Chinese producers and exporters. They charge that China's currency policy is intended to make its exports significantly less expensive, and its imports more expensive, than would occur if the RMB were a freely-traded currency. They argue that the RMB is significantly undervalued against the dollar and that this has been a major contributor to the large annual U.S. trade deficits with China and a significant decline in U.S. manufacturing jobs in recent years.

China began to peg the RMB to the dollar in 1994 at about 8.28 yuan (the base unit of the RMB) per dollar and kept the rate constant through July 2005, when, under pressure from its major trading partners, it moved to a managed peg system and began to allow the RMB to gradually appreciate over the next three years. In July 2008, China halted RMB appreciation because of the effects of the global economic crisis on

---

[*] This is an edited, reformatted and augmented version of a Congressional Research Service publication, CRS Report for Congress RS21625, dated July 22, 2013.

China's exporters. It resumed RMB appreciation in June 2010. From July 2005 through June 2013, the RMB appreciated by 34% on a nominal basis against the dollar and by 42% on a real (inflation-adjusted) basis. Over the past few years, China's current account surplus has declined, and its accumulation of foreign exchange reserves has slowed—factors that have led some analysts to contend the RMB is not as undervalued against the dollar as it once was.

The effects of China's currency policy on the U.S. economy are complex. If the RMB is undervalued (as some contend), then it might be viewed as an indirect export subsidy which artificially lowers the prices of Chinese products imported into the United States. Under this view, this benefits U.S. consumers and U.S. firms that use Chinese-made parts and components, but could negatively affect certain U.S. import-competing firms and their workers. An undervalued RMB might also have the effect of limiting the level of U.S. exports to China than might occur under a floating exchange rate system. The United States is also affected by China's large purchases of U.S. Treasury securities. China's intervention in currency markets causes it to accumulate large levels of foreign exchange reserves, especially U.S. dollars, which it then uses to purchase U.S. debt. Such purchases help the U.S. government fund its budget deficits and help keep U.S. interest rates low. These factors suggest that an appreciation of the RMB to the dollar benefits some U.S. economic sectors, but negatively affects others.

The effects of the recent global financial crisis have refocused attention on the need to reduce global imbalances in savings, investment, and trade, especially with regard to China and the United States, in order to avoid future crises. Many economists contend that China should take greater steps to rebalance its economy by lessening its dependence on exports and fixed investment as the main drivers of its economic growth, while boosting the level of domestic consumer demand (which would increase Chinese imports). A market-based currency policy is seen as an important factor in achieving this goal.

Currency bills aimed at addressing China's currency policy have been introduced in every session of Congress since 2003. The House approved a currency bill in the 111th Congress and the Senate passed one in the 112th Congress. Currency legislation has been proposed in the 113th Congress, including H.R. 1276 and S. 1114. In recent years, congressional concerns about undervalued currencies have moved beyond China to include those of several other countries as well.

INTRODUCTION AND OVERVIEW OF THE CURRENCY ISSUE

China's policy of intervention to limit the appreciation of its currency, the renminbi (RMB) against the dollar and other currencies has become a major source of tension with many of its trading partners, especially the United States.[1] Some analysts contend that China deliberately "manipulates" its currency in order to gain unfair trade advantages over its trading partners. They further argue that China's undervalued currency has been a major factor in the large annual U.S. trade deficits with China and has contributed to widespread job losses in the United States, especially in manufacturing. President Obama stated in February 2010 that China's undervalued currency puts U.S. firms at a "huge competitive disadvantage," and he pledged to make addressing China's currency policy a top priority.[2] At a news conference in November 2011, President Obama stated that China needed to "go ahead and move towards a market-based system for their currency" and that the United States and other countries felt that "enough is enough."[3]

Legislation to address China's currency policy has been introduced in every session of Congress since 2003. The House passed currency legislation in 2010 and the Senate did so in 2011, although none became law. On March 20, 2013, Representative Sander Levin introduced H.R. 1276 to "clarify that U.S. countervailing duties may be imposed to address subsidies relating to a fundamentally undervalued currency of any foreign country." On June 7, 2013, Senator Sherrod Brown introduced S. 1114, which would require action against certain misaligned currencies. In recent years, congressional concerns over misaligned (or undervalued currencies) have extended to other countries as well, leading some Members to propose that currency provisions be included in future U.S. trade agreements.

China began to gradually reform its currency policy in July 2005, and between then and the end of June 2013, the RMB has appreciated by 34% on a nominal basis (and 42% on an inflation- adjusted basis) against the U.S. dollar. In addition, China's trade surpluses have fallen sharply in recent years and its accumulation of foreign exchange reserves has slowed. These factors have led some analysts to conclude that the RMB exchange rate with the dollar may be approaching market levels, or is, at best, only modestly undervalued. However, other analysts contend that the RMB remains significantly undervalued against the dollar and complain that the RMB has appreciated little against the dollar since the end of 2011. Thus, they argue that continued pressure must be applied until the Chinese government adopts a market-based exchange rate.

Although economists differ as to the economic effects an undervalued RMB might have on the United States (many cite both positive and negative effects), most agree that greater currency flexibility by China would be one of several reforms that would help reduce global imbalances, which are believed to have been a major factor that sparked the global financial crisis and economic slowdown. They further contend that currency reform is in China's own long-term interests because it would boost economic efficiency. China's government has pledged to continue to make its currency policy more flexible, but has maintained that appreciating the RMB too quickly could cause significant job losses (especially in China's export sectors), which could disrupt the economy.

Some economists question whether RMB appreciation would produce significant net benefits for the U.S. economy. They argue that prices for Chinese products would rise, which would hurt U.S. consumers and U.S. firms that use imported Chinese components in their production. In addition, an appreciating RMB might lessen the Chinese government's need to purchase U.S. Treasury securities, which could cause U.S. interest rates to rise. It is further argued that an appreciating currency would do little to shift manufacturing done by foreign-invested firms (including U.S. firms) in China to the United States; instead, such firms would likely shift production to other low-cost East Asian countries. Finally, it is argued that an appreciating RMB might boost some U.S. exports to China, but the effects of lower prices for U.S. products in China could be negated to a large extent by China's restrictive trade and investment barriers. Such analysts view currency reform as part of a broad set of goals that U.S. trade policy should pursue. These goals include inducing China to rebalance its economy by making consumer demand, rather than exports and fixed investment, the main sources of China's economic growth; eliminate industrial policies that seek to promote and protect Chinese firms (especially state-owned firms); reduce trade and investment barriers; and improve protection of U.S. intellectual property rights.

This report provides an overview of the economic issues surrounding the current debate over China's currency policy. It identifies the economic costs and benefits of China's currency policy for both China and the United States, and possible implications if China were to allow its currency to significantly appreciate or to float freely. It also examines legislative proposals that seek to address China's (and other countries') currency policy.

BACKGROUND ON CHINA'S CURRENCY POLICY

Prior to 1994, China maintained a dual exchange rate system. This consisted of an official fixed exchange rate system (which was used by the government), and a relatively market-based exchange rate system that was used by importers and exporters in "swap markets,"[4] although access to foreign exchange was highly restricted in order to limit imports, resulting in a large black market for foreign exchange. The two exchange rates differed significantly. The official exchange rate with the dollar in 1993 was 5.77 yuan versus 8.70 yuan in the swap markets. China's dual exchange rate system was criticized by the United States because of the restrictions it (and other policies) placed on foreign imports.

In 1994, the Chinese government unified the two exchange rate systems at an initial rate of 8.70 yuan to the dollar, which eventually was allowed to rise to 8.28 by 1997 and was then kept relatively constant until July 2005. The RMB became largely convertible on a current account (trade) basis, but not on a capital account basis, meaning that foreign exchange in China is not regularly obtainable for investment purposes.[5] From 1994 until July 2005, China maintained a policy of pegging the RMB to the U.S. dollar at an exchange rate of roughly 8.28 yuan to the dollar. The peg appears to have been largely intended to promote a relatively stable environment for foreign trade and investment in China (since such a policy prevents large swings in exchange rates)—a policy utilized by many developing countries in their early development stages. The Chinese central bank maintained this peg by buying (or selling) as many dollar-denominated assets in exchange for newly printed yuan as needed to eliminate excess demand (supply) for the yuan. As a result, the exchange rate between the RMB and the dollar varied little, despite changing economic factors which could have otherwise caused the yuan to appreciate (or depreciate) relative to the dollar. Under a floating exchange rate system, the relative demand for the two countries' goods and assets would determine the exchange rate of the RMB to the dollar.

2005: China Reforms the Peg

The Chinese government modified its currency policy on July 21, 2005. It announced that the RMB's exchange rate would become "adjustable, based on market supply and demand with reference to exchange rate movements of currencies in a basket,"[6] and that the exchange rate of the U.S. dollar against the RMB would be adjusted from 8.28 yuan to 8.11, an appreciation of 2.1%. Unlike a true floating exchange rate, the RMB would be allowed to fluctuate by up to 0.3% (later changed to 0.5%) on a daily basis against the basket.

After July 2005, China allowed the RMB to appreciate steadily, but very slowly. From July 21, 2005, to July 21, 2008, the dollar-RMB exchange rate went from 8.11 to 6.83, an appreciation of 18.7% (or 20.8% if the initial 2.1% appreciation of the RMB to the dollar is included). The situation at this time might be best described as a "managed float"—market forces determined the general direction of the RMB's movement, but the government retarded its rate of appreciation through market intervention.

2008: RMB Appreciation Halted

China halted its currency appreciation policy around mid-July 2008 (see **Figure 1**), mainly because of declining global demand for Chinese products that resulted from the effects of the global financial crisis. In 2009, Chinese exports fell by 15.9% over the previous year. The Chinese government reported that thousands of export-oriented factories were shut down and that over 20 million migrant workers lost their jobs in 2009 because of the direct effects of the global economic slowdown.[7] In response, the Chinese government intervened to prevent any further appreciation of the RMB to the dollar. The RMB/dollar exchange rate was held relatively constant at 6.83 through around mid-June 2010.

2010: RMB Appreciation Resumes

On June 19, 2010, China's central bank, the People's Bank of China (PBC), stated that, based on current economic conditions, it had decided to "proceed further with reform of the RMB exchange rate regime and to enhance the RMB exchange rate flexibility." It ruled out any large one-time revaluations, stating "it is important to avoid any sharp and massive fluctuations of the RMB exchange rate," in part so that Chinese corporations could more easily adjust (such as through technology upgrading) to an appreciation of the currency. Many observers contend the timing of the RMB announcement was intended in part to prevent China's currency policy from being a central focus of the G-20 summit in Toronto in June 2010. As indicated in **Figure 2**, the RMB's exchange rate with the dollar has gone up and down since RMB appreciation was resumed, but overall, it has appreciated.[8] From June 19, 2010, (when appreciation was resumed) to July 10, 2013, the yuan/dollar exchange rate went from 6.83 to 6.17, an appreciation of 10.7%. Most of the appreciation occurred in 2010 and 2011. From January 1, 2012, to July 10, 2013, the RMB appreciated by only 2.1% against the dollar.[9] **Figure 3** shows the annual percentage change in the RMB's value against the dollar from 2001 to 2012 and indicates that the sharpest appreciation occurred in 2008 when it rose by 9.4%.

Factoring in Inflation and Trade-Weighted Flows

Some economists contend that a more accurate measurement of the yuan/dollar exchange rate involves accounting for differences in inflation between China and the United States—the real exchange rate. This approach is relevant because if prices are rising faster in China than in the United States, then the prices of Chinese tradable goods may be rising as well (even with no change in the nominal exchange rate). In effect, a higher Chinese inflation rate relative to the United States acts as a de facto appreciation of the RMB. From June 2005 to June 2013, China's consumer price inflation was about 31% higher than the U.S. level. Factoring in inflation into the RMB/dollar exchange rate indicates that the RMB appreciated in real terms by 42% during this period (as opposed to a 34% increase on a nominal basis).[10]

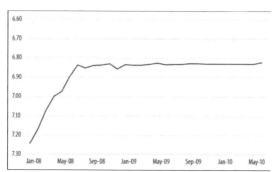

Source: Global Insight.
Note: Chart inverted for illustrative purposes. A rising line indicates appreciation of
   the RMB to the dollar and a falling line indicates depreciation.

Figure 1. Nominal RMB/Dollar Exchange Rate: January 2008 to May 2010 (yuan per U.S. dollar [monthly averages]).

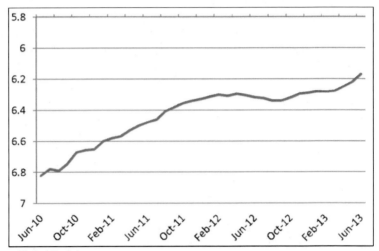

Source: Global Insight.

Notes: Chart inverted for illustrative purposes to show the appreciation or depreciation of the RMB against the dollar. Data are the Chinese government's official middle rate.

Figure 2. Average Monthly Yuan-Dollar Exchange Rates: June 2010-June 2013 (yuan per U.S. dollar).

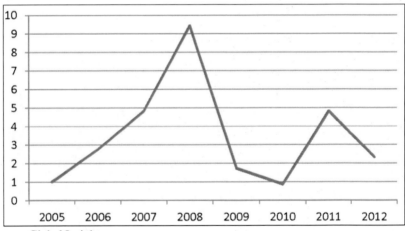

Source: Global Insight.
Notes: Change in average annual exchange rates.

Figure 3. Annual Percent Change in the Yuan/Dollar Exchange Rate: 2005 to 2012 (percent).

China's Currency Policy: An Analysis of the Economic Issues

A broader measurement of the RMB's movement involves looking at exchange rates with China's major trading partners by using a trade-weighted index (i.e., a basket of currencies) that is adjusted for inflation, often referred to as the "effective exchange rate."[11] The Bank of International Settlements maintains such an index for major economies, based on their trade with 61 trading partners.[12] Such an index is useful because it reflects overall changes in a country's exchange rate with its major trading partners as a whole—not just the United States. China's relative peg to the dollar has meant that as the dollar has depreciated or appreciated against a number of major currencies, the RMB has depreciated or appreciated against them as well. For example, from July 2008 to May 2010, when the RMB exchange rate to the dollar was kept constant (at 6.83 yuan per dollar), the real trade-weighted exchange rate index of China's currency (based on its trade with 61 major economies) appreciated by 8.2%. Between June 2010 (when appreciation of the RMB to the dollar was resumed) and May 2013, China's real trade- weighted exchange rate appreciated by 16.9%; and during the first five months of 2013, it rose by 4.6% (see **Figure 4**).[13]

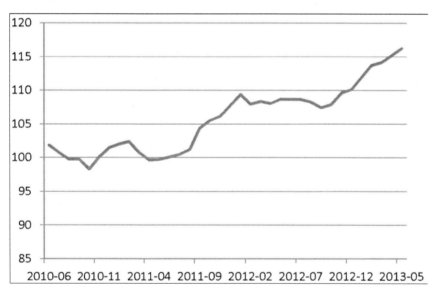

Source: Bank of International Settlements.
Note: Weights calculated based on China's trade with 61 economies. Inflation calculated using measurements of national consumer price indexes.

Figure 4. Change in China's Real Trade-Weighted Exchange Rate: June 2010-May 2013 (Index based on average annual 2005 data [2010 = 100]).

Concerns in the United States over China's Currency Policy: Trade Deficits and Jobs

Many U.S. policymakers and certain business and labor representatives have charged that the Chinese government "manipulates" its currency in order to make it significantly undervalued vis- à-vis the U.S. dollar, thus making Chinese exports to the United States less expensive, and U.S. exports to China more expensive, than they would be if exchange rates were determined by market forces.[14] They further contend that, while a pegged currency may have been appropriate during China's early stages of economic development, it can no longer be justified, given the size of China's economy and trade flows, and the impact these have on the global economy.[15]

Critics have further charged that the undervalued currency has been a major factor behind the burgeoning U.S. trade deficit with China, which grew from $84 billion in 2000 to $315 billion in 2012 and is projected to reach $325 billion in 2013 (based on data for January-May 2013). Other factors that have been cited as evidence of Chinese currency manipulation (and misalignment) have been China's massive accumulation of foreign exchange reserves and the size of its current account surpluses.[16] China is by far the world's largest holder of foreign exchange reserves. These grew from $212 billion in 2001 to $3.3 trillion in 2012 (year-end values).

Many analysts contend that large increases in China's foreign exchange reserves reflect the significance of Chinese intervention in currency markets to hold down the value of the RMB, which, they argue, has been a major factor behind China's large annual current account surpluses. According to one economist, a country's current account balance increases between 60 and 100 cents for each dollar spent on currency intervention.[17] As can be seen in **Figure 5**, China's foreign exchange holdings grew significantly from 2004 to 2011, averaging $363 billion in new reserves each year, but that growth slowed sharply in 2012 ($129 billion). As indicated in **Figure 6**, the annual rate of increase (percent change) in China's foreign exchange reserves went from a 51.3% rise in 2004, to 27.2% in 2008, to 4.1% in 2012.[18]

China's current account surplus rose from $69 billion in 2004 to a historical peak of $421 billion in 2008. It then declined over the next few years, dropping to $140 billion by 2011; it rose to $192 billion in 2012, according to the International Monetary Fund (IMF).[19] More significantly, China's current account surplus as a percent of GDP fell as well. It dropped from a historical high of 10.1% in 2007 to 1.9% in 2011, but increased to 2.3% in 2012.[20] In addition, China's exports of goods and services as a percent of

GDP declined from a historical high of 38.3% in 2007 to 27.5% in 2012, as indicated in **Figure 7**.

Many analysts contend the sharp drop in China's current account surpluses may have had more to do with the effects of the global economic slowdown (which greatly diminished global demand for Chinese products and led to a fall in foreign direct investment in China) than a change in China currency policies (although other Chinese economic policies were a major factor in the decline of the current account surplus, such as government policies to boost fixed investment and consumption which were employed to maintain rapid economic growth in the face of the global economic crisis).[21] In a July 2010 report, the IMF warned that, over the medium term, there was potential for China's sizable current account surpluses to return once its stimulus measures wound down and the global economy began to recover.[22] In July 2012, the IMF stated that, although the fall of China's current account surplus was a welcome sign, the external rebalancing was achieved at the cost of rising internal imbalances—namely the high rate of investment spending, which, the IMF assessed, would be difficult to sustain.[23]

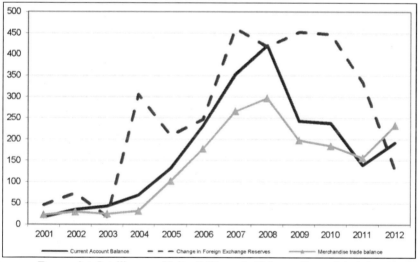

Source: Economist Intelligence Unit, IMF, and Chinese State Administration of Foreign Exchange.

Figure 5. China's Current Account Balance, Merchandise Trade Balance, and Annual Change in Foreign Exchange Reserves: 2001-2012 ($ billions).

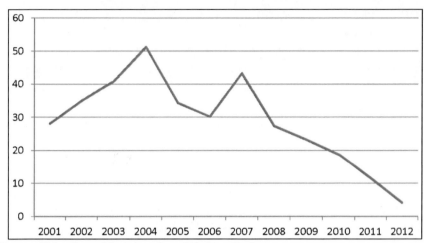

Source: China State Administration of Foreign Exchange.
Notes: Percent change over the previous year.

Figure 6. Annual Percent Change in China's Foreign Exchange Reserves: 2001-2012 (percent).

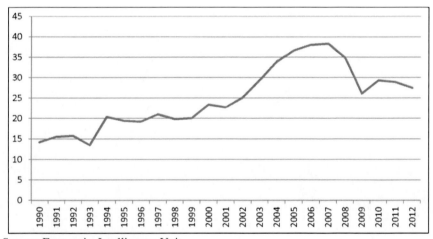

Source: Economist Intelligence Unit.

Figure 7. Chinese Exports of Goods and Services as a Percent of GDP: 1990-2012 (percent).

CONGRESSIONAL CONCERNS OVER CURRENCIES EXTENDS BEYOND CHINA

China is not alone in being accused of having an undervalued currency. Several other countries have been accused of attempting to keep the value of their currencies low through different efforts, including monetary policy.

A July 2012 study by the Peterson Institute for International Economics contends that "currency manipulation," based on "excessive" levels of foreign exchange reserves (FERs), is widespread, especially in developing and newly industrialized countries.[24] The study identified 22 economies that "manipulate their currency" based on the size of their FERs as a percent of GDP and the cumulative increase in FERs as a percent of GDP in 2012, the most significant of which were China (considered by the authors to be the most significant in terms of the size of China's economy and its FERs and the amounts of intervention), Denmark, Hong Kong, Korea, Malaysia, Singapore, Switzerland, and Taiwan.[25] The Peterson Institute estimated that currency intervention by the 22 economies increased the U.S. trade and current account deficits by $200 billion to $500 billion and caused the loss of 1 million to 5 million U.S. jobs.

In September 2012, Representative Mike Michaud sent a letter to Administration officials expressing "concern about Korea's ongoing intervention in its currency and its impact on U.S. businesses and workers, particularly now that the Korea-U.S. Free Trade Agreement (FTA) has been implemented. The undervaluation of the won already gives Korean exports a competitive advantage over U.S.-made goods, and if left unchecked it will neutralize Korean tariff reductions included in the agreement."

Japanese policies to boost economic growth, including quantitative easing (i.e., monetary expansion) have contributed to a sharp decline of the yen in international markets and have come under criticism by policymakers in several countries, In March 2013, Gao Xiqing, head of the China Investment Corporation (China's largest sovereign wealth fund), reportedly warned Japan against using its neighbors as a "garbage bin" by deliberately devaluating the yen through the use of expansive monetary policy.[26]

At a March 2013 Senate Finance Hearing on trade policy, Senator Debbie Stabenow stated that an agreement to include Japan in the Trans-Pacific Partnership (TPP) negotiations should include rules to counteract currency manipulation by Japan. She stated: "I want to indicate for the record that unless we see changes on currency manipulation and efforts and benchmarks to Japan opening their markets, I can't imagine why would we want to proceed with a one-sided agreement as it relates to American manufacturing and the automobile industry."[27] On April 12, 2013, Representative Levin, reacting to the Administration's announcement on Japan's participation in the Trans-Pacific Partnership, stated that "the absence of any mention of currency is highly problematical. Japan has used currency intervention to give Japanese auto companies one of their most significant unfair competitive advantages, adding tens of billions of dollars to their operating profits for every one-yen drop against the dollar."[28] While economic theory predicts that quantitative easing would cause a country's exchange rate to depreciate, it should be noted that it has been used in many countries following the financial crisis, including the United States.

In a May 2013 lecture, C. Fred Bergsten from the Peterson Institute stated that the international monetary system "now faces a clear and present danger: currency wars. Virtually every major country is seeking depreciation, or at least non-appreciation, of its currency to strengthen its economy and create jobs."[29]

A June 6, 2013, letter to the Obama Administration from 230 House Members on the TPP stated that it was "imperative" that the agreement address currency manipulation which has "contributed to the U.S. trade deficit and cost us American jobs."[30]

The current high rate of unemployment in the United States appears to have intensified concerns over the perceived impact of China's currency policy on the U.S. economy, especially employment. Many have argued that RMB appreciation would boost the level of U.S. jobs. Some analysts contend that there is a direct correlation between the U.S. trade deficit and U.S. job losses. For example, a 2012 study by the Economic Policy Institute (EPI) claims that the U.S. trade deficit with China (which EPI claims is largely the result of China's currency policy) led to the loss or displacement of 2.7 million jobs (of which, 77% were in manufacturing) between 2001 and 2011.[31] The EPI report states that, while U.S. exports to China support U.S. jobs, U.S. imports from China "displace American workers who would have been employed making these products in the United States."[32] Claims about the

China's Currency Policy: An Analysis of the Economic Issues   55

negative effect of China's exchange rate on U.S. employment and trade are often juxtaposed with the observation that China's economy has grown rapidly over the past five years (real GDP grew at an average annual rate of 9.2% from 2008 to 2012), while other countries have experienced slow or stagnant growth since the beginning of the global financial crisis. This has led some commentators to argue that China's exchange rate intervention represents a "beggar thy neighbor" policy (i.e., meant to promote Chinese economic development at the expense of other countries). (The validity of claims about the RMB's effect on the U.S. economy will be analyzed in the section below entitled "An Economic Analysis of the Effects of China's Currency ") For example, U.S. economist Paul Krugman in 2009 argued that the undervalued RMB had become a significant drag on global economic recovery, estimating that it had lowered global GDP by 1.4%, and had especially hurt poor countries.[33] Because of these factors, some Members have argued that China should be cited by the Department of the Treasury as a country that manipulates its currency in order to gain an unfair trade advantage (see text box).

IS CHINA A "CURRENCY MANIPULATOR?"

The U.S. Department of the Treasury is required on a biannual basis to issue a *Report to Congress on International Economic and Exchange Rate Policies* of major U.S. trading partners,[34] and to "consider whether countries manipulate the rate of exchange between their currency and the United States dollar for purposes of preventing effective balance of payments adjustments or gaining unfair competitive advantage in international trade."[35] If such manipulation is found to exist with respect to countries that have material global current account surpluses and have significant bilateral trade surpluses with the United States, the Secretary of the Treasury is directed to initiate negotiations with such countries on an expedited basis in the International Monetary Fund or bilaterally, for the purpose of ensuring that such countries regularly and promptly adjust the rate of exchange between their currencies and the U.S. dollar to permit effective balance of payments adjustments and to eliminate the unfair advantage. China was cited as a currency manipulator five times by Treasury from May 1992 and July 1994 over such issues as its dual exchange rate system, periods of currency devaluation, restrictions on imports, and lack of access to foreign exchange by importers.

Many Members of Congress have expressed frustration that Treasury has not cited China as a currency manipulator in recent years.[36] Observers note that the language in the statute is somewhat unclear as to what policies constitute actual currency manipulation (and the extent of Treasury's discretion to make such a determination). A 2005 Treasury Department report stated that such a determination under the guiding statute was "inherently difficult" because of the interplay of macroeconomic and microeconomic forces throughout the world, but said that such a designation could be made if the authorities of an economy "intentionally act to set the exchange rate at levels, or ranges, such that for a protracted period the exchange rate differs significantly from the rate that would have prevailed in the absence of action by the authorities."[37]

A 2005 Government Accountability Office (GAO) report on the Treasury Department's currency reports stated that in order for Treasury to reach a positive determination of currency manipulation, a country would have to have a material global current account surplus and a significant bilateral trade surplus with the United States, and would have to be manipulating its currency with the "intent" of gaining a trade advantage. Some observers contend that Treasury will not cite China as a currency manipulator because it cannot prove that China's currency policy is "intended" to give it an unfair trade advantage, since Chinese government intervention in currency markets attempts to slow or halt the appreciation of the RMB (as opposed to sharply depreciating the RMB). Other observers contend that as long as China continues to take steps to make its currency more flexible, Treasury will refrain from citing China. A third theory states that citing China as a currency manipulator would have no practical effect (especially since China and the United States are already engaged on this issue at the highest government level) other than to "name and shame," a policy that could anger the Chinese government without producing any concrete results. However, some U.S. policy analysts and Members of Congress have strongly urged the Treasury Department to designate China as a currency manipulator in order to "name and shame it." By doing so, it is argued, the United States would be sending a message that it was no longer willing to tolerate China's currency policy and it could encourage other countries to rally behind the U.S. position (including within the IMF, which exercises surveillance of its members currency policies), and could possibly lead to multilateral meeting/agreement on global exchange rate realignment.[38]

> Several bills have been introduced in Congress over the past few years that would attempt to limit the Treasury Department's discretion in taking action on undervalued currencies by requiring it to identify certain misaligned currencies, based on specific criteria, regardless of intent of the currency policy.

Legislative Proposals to Address Undervalued Currencies

Numerous bills have been introduced in Congress over the past several years that have sought to induce China (and other countries) to reform its currency policy or to address the perceived effects of that policy on the U.S. economy. For example, one bill introduced in the 108th Congress by Senator Schumer (S. 1586) sought to impose additional duties of 27.5% on imported Chinese products unless China appreciated its currency to market levels. The House approved a currency bill (H.R. 2378) in the 111th Congress and the Senate passed one (S. 1619) in the 112th Congress, though neither became law.

Over the past few years, some legislative proposals have sought to apply U.S. anti-dumping and countervailing duty measures to address the effects of China's undervalued currency, namely to treat it as an export subsidy (countervailing measures) or as a factor that is included in the determination of anti-dumping duties. This would likely increase U.S. countervailing and anti-dumping duties on certain imports from China. A major source of contention is whether such measures would be consistent with U.S. obligations in the World Trade Organization (WTO). Some contend that the WTO allows countries (under certain conditions) to administer their own trade remedy laws, and thus they argue that making currency undervaluation a factor in determining countervailing or anti-dumping duties would be consistent with WTO rules. Critics of such proposals counter that WTO rules do not specifically include currency undervaluation as a factor that can be used to implement trade remedy actions, and thus, such proposals, if enacted, might be challenged by China (and possibly other WTO members) as a violation of WTO rules.[39]

Another major objective of various recent currency bills is to eliminate current provisions of U.S. trade laws that require the Treasury Department to identify countries that intentionally "manipulate" their currency. Treasury has not identified any country for manipulating its currency since 1994. Some bills have sought to create a process whereby Treasury would identify countries with currencies that were estimated to be fundamentally misaligned (based on certain criteria), regardless of intent. Such bills list a number of actions (some of which would be punitive) the U.S. government would be directed to take against certain "priority" countries.

Some supporters of currency legislation aimed at China hope that the introduction of such bills will induce China to appreciate its currency more rapidly. Opponents of the bills contend that such legislation could antagonize China and induce it to slow the rate of RMB appreciation. Another concern of opponents is that China might also retaliate against U.S. exports to China and/or U.S.-invested firms in China if such legislation became law.

Legislation in the 113th Congress

H.R. 1276: The Currency Reform for Fair Trade Act

H.R. 1276 was introduced by Representative Sander Levin on March 20, 2013. The bill is identical to the one he introduced in the 112th Congress (H.R. 639) and nearly identical to H.R. 2378, which passed the House during the 111th Congress by a vote of 284 to 123.

H.R. 1276 would seek to clarify certain provisions of U.S. countervailing duty laws (pertaining to foreign government export subsidies) that would allow the Commerce Department to consider a "fundamentally misaligned currency" as an actionable subsidy.[40] For example, it would clarify that a fundamentally undervalued currency could be treated by the Commerce Department as a benefit conferred by a foreign government to its exports.[41] In addition, the bill seeks to clarify that, in the case of a subsidy relating to a fundamentally undervalued currency, the fact that the subsidy (i.e., the undervalued currency) may have also benefitted non-exporting firms (in addition to exporting firms), would not, for that reason alone, mean that the undervalued currency was not an actionable subsidy under U.S. countervailing duty law.[42] The bill would direct the Commerce Department to use, if possible, data and methodologies utilized by the International Monetary Fund (IMF) to estimate real effective exchange rate undervaluation.

Factors that would be used by the Commerce Department to determine if a country's currency is fundamentally undervalued for the purposes of U.S. countervailing duty laws would include (over an 18-month period): (1) protracted and large-scale intervention in currency markets; (2) a real effective exchange rate estimated to be undervalued by at least 5%; and (3) foreign asset reserves held by the government that exceed: (A) the amount needed to repay its debt obligations over the next year; (B) 20% of the nation's money supply; and (C) the value of the country's imports over the previous four months.

The bill would direct the Commerce Department to estimate the "subsidy" relating to a fundamentally undervalued currency for the purpose of imposing countervailing duties, which would be defined as the difference between a currency's real effective exchange rate and its equilibrium real effective exchange rate.[43] The bill further directs Commerce (when appropriate) to use the simple average of the methodologies used by the IMF's Consultative Group on Exchange Rates. If such data are not available from the IMF, Commerce would be directed to use generally accepted economic and econometric techniques and methodologies to measure the level of undervaluation.

S. 1114: The Currency Exchange Rate Oversight Reform Act of 2013

S. 1114 was introduced by Senator Sherrod Brown on June 7, 2013. It is essentially the same bill (S. 1619) that Senator Brown introduced in 2011 and was passed by the Senate on October 11, 2011. The bill would provide for the identification of fundamentally misaligned currencies and require action to correct the misalignment for certain "priority" countries. The bill would require the Treasury Department to issue a semiannual report to Congress on international monetary policy and currency exchange rates, which, in addition to several provisions under current law,[44] would include:

- a description of any currency intervention by the United States or other major economies or trading partners of the United States, or other actions undertaken to adjust the actual exchange rate relative to the U.S. dollar;
- an evaluation of the domestic and global factors that underlie the conditions in the currency markets;
- with respect to currencies of countries with significant trade flows with the United States and other major global currencies, a determination and designation by Treasury as to which of these are in fundamental misalignment;
- a list of currencies designated for "priority action";
- an identification of the nominal value associated with the medium-term equilibrium exchange rate relative to the U.S. dollar for each currency listed for priority action; and

- a description of any consultations conducted, including any actions taken to eliminate the fundamental misalignment.

Treasury would be required to seek negotiations with countries designated for priority action. Factors used to determine priority countries would include those that are (1) engaging in protracted large-scale intervention in currency markets, particularly if accompanied by monetary sterilization measures; (2) engaging in excessive and prolonged accumulation of foreign exchange reserves for balance of payment (BOP) purposes; (3) introducing or modifying restrictions or incentives (for balance of payment purposes) on capital inflows and outflows that are inconsistent with the goal of achieving full currency convertibility; and (4) pursuing any other policy or action that the Treasury Secretary views as warranting designation for priority action.

If a country that has a currency designated for priority action fails to eliminate the fundamental misalignment within 90 days, the following would occur:

- In antidumping duty investigations, the Commerce Department would be required to factor in the estimated level of currency undervaluation when comparing the export price with the normal value (i.e., the exporter's home market value) when determining the level of dumping that may have taken place. This could raise the level of anti-dumping duties imposed on imports.
- The President would be required to prohibit the procurement by the federal government of products or services from the country unless it is a party to the World Trade Organization's Government Procurement Agreement (GPA). China is negotiating to join the GPA, but is currently not a member.
- The Overseas Private Investment Corporation (OPIC) would be prohibited from approving any new financing (including insurance, reinsurance, or guarantee) with respect to a project located within the country. This provision would not affect China because OPIC is already prohibited by U.S. law from operating in China.
- The U.S. Executive Director at each multilateral bank would be directed to oppose the approval of any new financing to the government of a country, or for a project located within that country.
- The United States would request the IMF to hold special consultations with the country on ways to eliminate the fundamental misalignment.

China's Currency Policy: An Analysis of the Economic Issues   61

If a country that has a currency designated for priority action fails to take steps to eliminate the fundamental misalignment within 360 days after its designation by Treasury, the following would occur:

- The U.S. Trade Representative (USTR) would be required to request consultations in the WTO (i.e., initiate a dispute settlement case) with the country regarding the consistency of the country's actions with its obligations in the WTO.
- The Treasury Secretary would be required to consult with the Board of Governors of the Federal Reserve System to consider undertaking remedial intervention in international currency markets in response to the fundamental misalignment of the designated currency and coordinating such intervention with other monetary authorities and the IMF.
- The Treasury Department would be required to oppose increasing the voting shares or representation in any international financial institution (such as the IMF) if the country in question would benefit from that change.

S. 1114 would also amend U.S. countervailing duty law to require the Commerce Department to initiate an investigation to determine whether currency undervaluation is providing, directly or indirectly, a countervailing subsidy if a petition is filed by an interested party and is accompanied by information supporting those allegations. The bill also seeks to clarify that, in the case of a subsidy relating to a fundamentally undervalued currency, the fact that the subsidy (i.e., the undervalued currency) may have also benefitted non-exporting firms would not, for that reason alone, mean that the subsidy could not be considered to be a measure that is contingent upon export performance. The bill includes waiver provisions for actions taken toward priority countries and a process for Congress to disapprove the waivers. S. 1114 would also add a provision to U.S. antidumping law that would require the Commerce Department to include whether a country has been designated as having a currency for priority action as a factor to be considered during a review of whether to change the designation of a non-market economy country to one that is a market economy country.[45]

For the purposes of measuring a benefit conferred by a misaligned currency in a regular countervailing duty case, Commerce would be directed to compare the simple average of the real exchange rates derived from the application of the IMF's equilibrium real exchange rate approach and the macroeconomic balance approach to the official daily exchange rate, relying on IMF or World Bank data, if available, or other international organizations or national governments if such data are not available. For a countervailing duty case involving a fundamentally misaligned currency for priority action, S. 1114 would direct Commerce to calculate the benefit of a misaligned currency by comparing the nominal value associated with the medium-term equilibrium exchange rate of the currency of the exporting country to the official daily exchange rate. For the purposes of antidumping duty cases involving a fundamentally misaligned currency for priority action, S. 1114 would require the Department of Commerce to adjust the price used to establish the export price or constructed export price to reflect the fundamental misalignment of the currency of the exporting country. Fundamental misalignment is defined as a significant and sustained undervaluation of the prevailing real effective exchange rate, adjusted for cyclical and transitory factors, from its medium-term equilibrium level. The term "fundamental misalignment" and measurements of misalignment in the bill appear to have been largely drawn from the IMF's 2007 Decision on Bilateral Surveillance over Members' Policies (see text box below).

THE IMF AND CURRENCY MISALIGNMENT

The IMF's 2007 Decision on Bilateral Surveillance over Members' Policies set new guidelines on exchange rate policies and identified certain developments that could affect global external stability, including exchange rate policies which in turn could trigger a thorough review by the IMF and possible consultations with an IMF member. Developments that could trigger a review include (1) protracted large-scale intervention in exchange markets; (2) official or quasi-official borrowing that is unsustainable or brings unduly high liquidity risks or excessive and prolonged accumulation of foreign assets for balance of payment purposes; (3) monetary and other financial policies that provide abnormal encouragement or discouragement to capital flows; (4) significant policies that restrict or provide incentives for capital flows or current transactions or payments; (5) large and prolonged current account deficits or surpluses; (6) large external sector vulnerabilities; and (7) fundamental exchange rate misalignment.

> A fundamental exchange rate misalignment may trigger IMF review when (1) there is a misalignment between the prevailing real effective exchange rate and the level that would bring the underlying current account in line with the equilibrium current account; (2) the misalignment is significant; (3) the significant misalignment is expected to persist under established exchange rate policies; and (4) the significant and persistent misalignment is established beyond any reasonable doubt. The equilibrium real effective exchange rate is defined as one that is consistent with an underlying current account (adjusted for temporary factors) that is estimated to be in line with economic fundamentals, (such as productivity differentials, the terms of trade, permanent shifts in factor endowments, demographics, and world interest rates), over the medium term.[46]

The Obama Administration's Position and Policies

President Obama stated in February 2010 that China's undervalued currency puts U.S. firms at a "huge competitive disadvantage," and he pledged to make addressing China's currency policy a top priority.[47] At a news conference in November 2011, President Obama stated that China needed to "go ahead and move towards a market-based system for their currency" and that the United States and other countries felt that "enough is enough."[48]

Administration officials have welcomed greater congressional involvement on the China currency issue as long as legislative proposals do not violate U.S. WTO obligations and do not complicate ongoing bilateral and multilateral negotiations with China on the issue. The Administration did not publicly indicate whether it supported or opposed the House-passed version of H.R. 2378 in the 111th Congress. During considering of S. 1619 by the Senate in October 2011, an Administration official stated:

> We share the goal of the legislation in taking action to ensure that our workers and companies have a more level playing field with China, including addressing the under- valuation of their currency, an issue that I've spoken about and certainly Secretary Geithner and others have spoken about. Aspects of the legislation do, as I've said, raise concerns about consistency with our international obligations, which is why we're in the process of discussing with Congress those issues. And if this legislation were to advance, we would expect those concerns to be addressed.[49]

The Obama Administration has sought to directly engage China on the currency issue through the Strategic & Economic Dialogue (S&ED) and the

Joint Commission on Commerce and Trade (JCCT).[50] At the end of the May 2011 S&ED session, then Secretary of the Treasury Tim Geithner stated: "We hope that China moves to allow the exchange rate to appreciate more rapidly and more broadly against the currencies of all its trading partners. And this adjustment, of course, is critical not just to China's ongoing efforts to contain inflationary pressures and to manage the risks that capital inflows bring to credit and asset markets, but also to encourage this broad shift to a growth strategy led by domestic demand."[51] At the May 2012 S&ED talks, Geithner acknowledged that China had made progress, stating: "China has acted to move toward a more flexible exchange rate system in which the market plays a greater role. It is intervening less in exchange markets. China is also moving to liberalize controls on the international use of its currency and on capital movements into and out of the country."[52] At the July 2013 S&ED session, China reiterated its commitment to move to a market-determined exchange rate.

It addition, the Obama Administration has sought to use multilateral channels, such as the Group of 20 (G-20) of leading economies and the IMF, as a means to boost international cooperation on external balances and exchange rate policies and to bring more pressure on China to appreciate its currency.[53] For example, on October 20, 2010, Secretary Geithner issued a proposal aimed at the G-20 meeting of finance ministers and central bank governors on October 23, 2010. The proposal contained three main points:[54]

- G-20 countries should commit to taking steps to reduce external imbalances (both surpluses and deficits) below a specified share of GDP over the next few years.
- G-20 countries should commit to refrain from exchange rate policies designed to achieve competitive advantage by either weakening their currency or preventing appreciation of an undervalued currency. G-20 emerging market countries with significantly undervalued currencies (and adequate precautionary foreign exchange reserves) need to allow their exchange rates to adjust fully over time to levels consistent with economic fundamentals. G-20 advanced economies should work to ensure against excessive volatility and disorderly movements in exchange rates.
- The G-20 should call on the IMF to assume a special role in monitoring progress on these commitments and should publish a semiannual report assessing progress the G-20 countries have made to achieve these goals.

China's Currency Policy: An Analysis of the Economic Issues 65

China and a number of other G-20 members, though supporting efforts to rebalance the global economy, opposed the idea of using numerical targets.

In February 2013, the G-7 finance ministers and central bank governors issued a statement reaffirming their "longstanding commitment to market-determined exchange rates" and that fiscal and monetary policies would remain oriented towards meeting domestic objectives, and that members would not target exchange rates. They noted that members agreed that excessive volatility and disorderly movements in exchange rates can have adverse implications for economic and financial stability.[55]

AN ECONOMIC ANALYSIS OF THE EFFECTS OF CHINA'S CURRENCY ON THE U.S. ECONOMY

This section examines a number of issues pertaining to the effects of China's undervalued currency on the U.S. economy. The economic effects on the Chinese economy of an undervalued currency are examined later in the report.

What Is the RMB's "True Value"? Can it Be Accurately Estimated?

A major question raised by U.S. policymakers is: what would the RMB's exchange rate with the dollar (and other currencies) be if China allowed its currency to float freely in international markets and did not intervene to affect the RMB's value and how does this compare to the current rate of exchange?[56] Such a question attempts to ascertain to what degree the RMB is misaligned or undervalued against the dollar. Several economic studies have been issued over the years that have attempted to estimate the degree of the RMB's undervaluation against the dollar with varying results. For example, four separate studies issued in 2009 concluded that the RMB was undervalued against the dollar by rates of 12%,[57] 25%,[58] 40%[59], and 50%,[60] respectively.

A 2006 Department of the Treasury report describes a number of challenges that arise from attempting to use economic models to predict market exchange rates. It notes that there is no single model that accurately explains exchange rate movements, that such models rarely, if ever, incorporate financial market flows, and that their conclusions can vary considerably, based on the variables used. However, the report stated that examining such models can produce useful information in understanding exchange rate movements if they focus only on serious misalignments; use real effective, not bilateral, exchange rates; utilize several different models, recognizing that no one model will provide precise answers; focus only on protracted misalignments where currency adjustments are not taking place; supplement judgments about misalignment with analysis of empirical data, indicators, policies, and institutional factors; and verify whether there are any market-based reasons for a currency's misalignment.[61]

The IMF appears to largely follow the approach outlined by the Treasury Department's report. The IMF's Consultative Group on Exchange Rates uses three different methodologies for its surveillance and assessment of the exchange rate regimes of its members, including an equilibrium real exchange rate (ERER) approach, an external sustainability (ES) approach, and the macroeconomic balance (MB) approach.[62] In July 2011, the IMF stated that it believed "that the renminbi remains substantially below the level consistent with medium-term fundaments."

For the first time, the IMF made public its estimates of the RMB's undervaluation, which included 3% under the ERER approach, 17% under the ES approach, and 23% under the MB approach.[63] However, an IMF report that described its three exchange rate methodologies cautioned:

> While adopting different empirical methodologies goes some way towards strengthening the robustness of exchange rate assessments, it should be recognized that such assessments are unavoidably subject to large margins of uncertainty. These relate to a number of factors, such as the potential instability of the underlying macroeconomic links, differences in these links across countries, significant measurement problems for some variables, as well as the imperfect "fit" of the models. Some of these problems may be more severe for emerging market economies, where structural change is more likely to play an important role and where limitations in terms of data availability and length of sample are more acute.[64]

In July 2012, the IMF declared that: "The renminbi is assessed to be moderately undervalued, reflecting a reassessment of the underlying current account, slower international reserves and in accumulation, and past real effective exchange rate appreciation."[65] The IMF gave a range of the RMB's undervaluation (described as the difference between the real effective exchange rate and the rate that would be "consistent with fundamentals and desirable policies") of 5%-10%.[66] In May 2013, the IMF repeated its assessment that the RMB remained moderately undervalued against a basket of currencies.[67]

Most studies of the RMB's projected market value against the dollar have involved one-time estimates made for a given period of time and thus may not reflect fundamental economic changes that may have subsequently occurred, which in turn would affect estimates of the RMB's equilibrium exchange rate with the dollar in other years. For example, a one-time study on China's exchange rate in 2009 will not reflect any change (appreciation or depreciation) in the currency that has occurred since the study was done. One exception to these limitations is partially addressed by work done by William R. Cline with the Peterson Institute for International economics, who has made estimates of the equilibrium exchange rates for a number of countries, including China, from 2008 to 2013 on a semiannual basis.[68]

Cline uses the fundamental equilibrium exchange rate (FEER) method to estimate exchange rates. One of the assumptions that he uses is that current account balances around the world are temporarily out of line with their "fundamental" value. Once an estimate has been made of what the fundamental current account balance should be, one can calculate how much the exchange rate must change in value to achieve that current account adjustment. To calculate the level of misevaluation for one country under this method, estimates of how far exchange rates for every country are out of equilibrium, including countries with floating exchange rates, must be made.

One of the main sources of contention in FEER estimates is choosing an "equilibrium" current account balance for each country. Estimates of the RMB's undervaluation are typically defined as the appreciation that would be required for China to attain "equilibrium" in its current account balance. But there is no consensus based on theory or evidence to determine what equilibrium would be, so a judgmental approach is used. Cline determines his own current account targets for different countries—for China the target is a current account surplus of no more than 3% of GDP while the target for the United States is a current account deficit that is no greater than 3% of GDP. The estimates of the RMB's undervaluation made by Cline utilize actual and projected data (such as GDP growth and current account balances) from the IMF's World Economic Outlook in order to calculate an equilibrium exchange rate. For example, Cline's May 2013 study used the IMF's projection for China's current account surplus as a percent of GDP in 2018 (4.0%) and estimates how much the RMB would need to appreciate against the dollar to obtain a current account surplus target goal that is 3% of GDP. As indicated in

Figure 8, Cline's estimates of the amount of appreciation the RMB would need to obtain equilibrium (i.e., a current account surplus of 3% of GDP) has fallen from a peak of 40.7% in December 2009 to 5.9% in October 2012; it rose to 6.0% for April 2013.

As noted earlier, Cline made FEER estimates relative to the dollar for a number of currencies, not just the RMB. His May 2013 study estimates the equilibrium level of the currencies of 33 countries plus the euro area. The top 10 countries with the most undervalued currencies as of April 2013 are listed in **Table 1** in ranking order.[69] The top five countries with the most undervalued currencies were Singapore (undervalued by 25.7%), Taiwan (18.8%), Sweden (13.4%), Japan (13.1%), and Switzerland (10.8%); China ranked ninth.

There is no universally accepted methodology for precisely determining a country's real market exchange rate. The economic conditions and assumptions that are used to determine "equilibrium" exchange rates change continuously. As a result, many analysts question their usefulness to U.S. policymakers, such as providing a precise U.S. goal for an appreciation of the RMB vis-a-vis dollar or for use in trade remedy legislation that would seek to offset the benefit ("subsidy") conferred by the RMB's undervaluation, such as through the use of countervailing or antidumping measures.

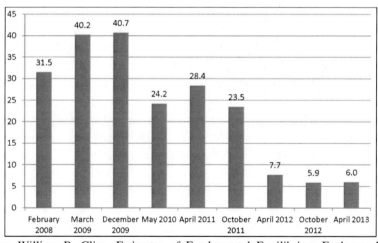

Source: William R. Cline, Estimates of Fundamental Equilibrium Exchange Rates, Peterson Institute for International Economics, various years.

Figure 8. Timeline of Estimates of the RMB's Undervaluation Relative to the Dollar Using the FEER Method: 2008-2013 (percent).

China's Currency Policy: An Analysis of the Economic Issues 69

Table 1. Estimates of Currency Misalignment Against the Dollar in April 2013 for Selected Countries (%)

Country	Estimated Percent Change in Exchange Rate Needed to Obtain an FEER-Consistent rate with the Dollar (%)
Singapore	25.7
Taiwan	18.8
Sweden	13.4
Japan	13.1
Switzerland	10.8
Hong Kong	8.7
Malaysia	6.5
The Philippines	6.1
China	**6.0**
Thailand	4.5

Source: Cline, William R., Peterson Institute for International Economics, *Estimates of Fundamental Equilibrium Exchange Rates*, May 2013.

The Debate over the Effects of Exchange Rate Appreciation on Trade Flows and the Deficit

Many policymakers might expect that if China significantly appreciated its currency, U.S. exports to China would rise, imports from China would fall, and the U.S. trade deficit would decline within a relatively short period of time. For example, C. Fred Bergsten from the Peterson Institute for International Economics argued in 2010 that a market-based RMB would lower the annual U.S. current account deficit by $100 billion to $150 billion.[70] But the issue of the possible effects of an RMB appreciation on the U.S. economy is complicated by the fact that there are short-term and long-term implications of RMB appreciation, and that exchange rates are but one of many factors that affect trade flows.

To illustrate that exchange rates are only one factor that determine trade flows, one can look at the effect of the 21% RMB appreciation of the RMB to the dollar from July 2005 to July 2008 on U.S.-China trade flows. On the one hand, during this period U.S. imports from China increased by 39%, compared to a 92% increase from 2001 to 2004 (when the exchange rate remained constant).[71] On the other hand, U.S. exports to China during the 2005-2008 period did not grow as fast as during the 2001-2004 period (71% versus 81%).[72] Despite the RMB's appreciation from 2005 to 2008, the U.S. trade deficit with China still rose by 30.1% (although the overall U.S. current account deficit declined by nearly 6%).[73] The appreciation of the RMB appears to have had little effect on China's overall trade balance from 2005 to 2008. During this time, China's merchandise trade surplus increased from $102 billion to $297 billion, an increase of 191%, and China's current account surplus and accumulation of foreign exchange reserves both increased by 165% over this period.

The J Curve Effect

Part of the problem in attempting to evaluate the effects of the RMB's appreciation is that it can take time (perhaps a few years) before changes in exchange rates are reflected in changes to prices of tradable goods and services, and, hence, result in changes to imports, exports, and trade balances. An appreciated RMB could actually worsen the U.S. trade deficit in the short run if the volume (demand) of imports from China did not decline at the same rate that prices increased (the so-called J-Curve effect). It would take time for U.S. consumers of higher-priced Chinese products to find lower-priced (non-Chinese) products or other alternatives and thus reduce overall demand for Chinese imports.[74] In addition, there would be a lag time in terms of the effects of an appreciated RMB on prices of Chinese products, since prices for many exports are set several months ahead of time in contracts. If an appreciated currency lowered prices for U.S. products, it could take time for increased Chinese demand to be signaled to U.S. producers and exporters and for them to boost production to meet the new demand. Over time, one would expect the effects of currency appreciation to affect the flow of bilateral trade and, possibly, produce a decrease in the bilateral trade imbalance (although the size of the overall U.S. trade deficit might not change because that is determined by a number of factors other than exchange rates).

The Role of Exchange Rate Pass-Through

Another factor to consider in evaluating the effects an RMB appreciation may have had on trade flows is to examine how price changes would be passed on or distributed. If the RMB appreciates against the dollar, not all of the price increase resulting from the appreciation may be passed on to the U.S. consumer. Some of it may be absorbed by Chinese laborers, producers, or exporters, and some by U.S. importers, wholesalers, or retailers. According to the U.S. Department of Labor, from 2003 to 2012 (year-end), the price index for U.S. imports from China rose by 6.1% (compared to a 19.2% rise in import prices for total U.S. imports of non-petroleum products) even the RMB appreciated in nominal terms by 33.7% over this period (see **Figure 9**).[75] This would suggest that only a small part of the increase in prices for Chinese products that might have resulted from the RMB's appreciation was passed on to U.S. consumers.[76] If prices are not completely passed through to consumers, then consumer demand for Chinese imports will fall less than if they were, all else equal.

China's Role in the Global Supply Chain

The issue of exchange rate effects is further complicated by China's role as a major assembly center for multinational corporations. Many analysts contend that the sharp increase in U.S. imports from China over the past several years (and hence the growing bilateral trade imbalance) is largely the result of movement in production facilities from other (primarily Asian) countries to China. That is, various products that used to be assembled in such places as Japan, Taiwan, Hong Kong, etc., and then exported to the United States are now being made in China (in many cases, by U.S. and other foreign firms in China) and exported to the United States. According to Chinese data, foreign-invested firms in China account for over half of China's trade flows (both exports and imports). Such firms import raw materials, intermediate goods (such as components), and production machinery to China. One study of Apple Inc.'s iPod found that the product itself was assembled in China in factories owned by a Taiwanese company from components that were produced by numerous multinational corporations. The level of value added by Chinese workers who assembled the iPod in China was estimated to be small relative to the total cost of producing each unit (about 3%), and much smaller relative to the retail price of the unit sold in the United States.[77] Some analysts contend that, because of the high level of imported inputs that comprise a large share of China's exports, an appreciated RMB would have little effect on the prices of Chinese exports, and hence have little effect on bilateral trade flows. Others contend that, even if foreign-invested firms in China faced significantly higher costs because of an appreciated RMB, they would move production to another low-cost country, and thus, while the U.S trade deficit with China decreased, the U.S. trade deficit with other countries would increase.

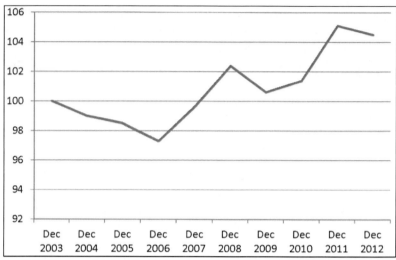

Source: U.S. Bureau of Labor Statistics.
Note: 2003 is the first available year for data on import prices of Chinese commodities.

Figure 9. Index of U.S. Import Prices of Commodities from China: December 2003-December 2012 (2003=100).

Underlying Macroeconomic Imbalances Are Unlikely to Disappear

By accounting identity, the overall trade deficit is equal to the shortfall between domestic saving and investment, while an overall trade surplus is equal to a surplus of domestic saving relative to investment. For many years, China has been a high-saving country that has run overall trade surpluses and the United States has been a low-saving country that has run overall trade deficits (for more discussion on this issue, see **Appendix**). China's use of an exchange rate peg and capital controls may have contributed to its high saving rate, but it is unlikely that movement to a floating exchange rate would eliminate the large disparity between U.S. and Chinese saving rates. Thus, it is likely that the United States would continue to be a net debtor and China would continue to be a net creditor if the RMB rose in value. If so, economic theory predicts the countries' bilateral trade imbalance would either persist or possibly be replaced by new bilateral imbalances with third countries.

Differing Opinions on Making RMB Appreciation a Top U.S. Trade Priority

As noted earlier, a number of U.S. economists have argued that China's undervalued currency has negatively affected the U.S. and global economies.

China's Currency Policy: An Analysis of the Economic Issues 73

However, other economists contend that, while an undervalued RMB may have distorted trade flows to some extent, it is not the most significant challenge to U.S. economic interests vis-à-vis China, and therefore, they argue, an appreciation of the currency by itself would do little to boost the U.S. economy. For example,

- Derek Scissors at the Heritage Foundation contends that appreciation of the RMB would have little impact on U.S. employment, stating it would create "a few thousand jobs at best."[78] He argues that the Chinese government's extensive use of industrial policies, namely subsidies and regulatory protection (such as state- sponsored monopolies), sharply limits imports of goods and services that compete with the state sector, which would remain unaffected even if the RMB were appreciated. He notes: "Guaranteed revenue and economies of scale make state firms modestly competitive as exporters when they would otherwise be uncompetitive. The real harm, however, is to imports of goods and services from the U.S. The degree of state predominance caps the total share available to all domestic private and foreign companies, leaving American producers in a vicious battle for permanently minor market segments. This is a far more stringent limitation than an undervalued currency."[79]
- Michael Pettis with the Carnegie Endowment for International Peace makes a similar argument except that he contends that Chinese government "financial repression" policies have kept real returns to deposits low (and sometimes negative) in China in order to keep real lending rates artificially low (since they are set by the government, not market conditions) for Chinese firms (especially state-owned firms). He states that this constitutes a forced transfer of income from Chinese households to Chinese producers, which has led to over-investment and over-capacity by Chinese firms, with much of that excess capacity being exported. Pettis concludes that "as long as China continues to subsidize its production growth at the expense of household income, it will have difficulty increasing domestic demand and cutting its reliance on exports."[80]
- A study by the Federal Reserve Bank of San Francisco contends that, although the United States is running record trade deficits with China, the level of imports from China relative to U.S. GDP and U.S. personal consumption expenditures is relatively small.[81] According to the study, U.S. imports of goods and services from China accounted

for 2.5% of GDP in 2010, and these imports accounted for only 2.7% of U.S. personal expenditures for goods and services in 2010.[82] The study estimated that on average for every one dollar that is spent in the United States on a product that is labeled "made in China," 55 cents goes for services supplied in the United States, such as transportation, wholesale, and retail. As a result, according to the study, the actual value of goods and services originating in China totaled only 1.2% of U.S. personal expenditures in 2010; accounting for the level of imported intermediate inputs from China that are used to manufacture goods that are labeled "made in the USA" would raise this level to 1.9%. Some argue that the Federal Reserve Bank study illustrates that U.S. imports from China do not necessarily displace U.S. workers (and in fact, support U.S. jobs in a number of sectors) and that RMB appreciation would likely have little effect on the U.S. economy.

Winners and Losers of RMB Appreciation from an Economic Perspective

Economists generally oppose the use of policies (such as subsidies and trade protection) that interrupt market forces and distort the most efficient distribution of resources. A fixed or managed float exchange rate whose level is not adjusted when economic conditions change might be viewed as such a distortion.[83] Thus, from an economist's perspective, adopting a more market-based currency would likely be a win-win situation for China, the United States, and the global economy as a whole, in the sense that it would lead to a more efficient allocation of resources in both countries (though not necessarily any effect on overall employment levels, as discussed below). From a policy perspective, it could be argued that China's current undervalued currency produces economic "winners and losers" in both countries, and therefore, an adjustment to that policy would produce a new set of economic "winners and losers." Although numerous factors affect global economic growth and trade flows, let us assume that an appreciation of the RMB produces a significant change in trade. What would the effects be for the U.S. economy?

Effect on U.S Exporters and Import-Competitors
When exchange rate policy causes the RMB to be less expensive than it would be if it were determined by supply and demand, it causes Chinese

exports to be relatively inexpensive and U.S. exports to China to be relatively expensive. As a result, U.S. exports and the production of U.S. goods and services that compete with Chinese imports fall, in the short run.[84] Many of the affected firms are in the manufacturing sector.[85] This causes the trade deficit to rise and reduces aggregate demand in the short run, all else equal. A market-based exchange rate could boost U.S. exports and provide some relief to U.S. firms that directly compete with Chinese firms.

Effect on U.S. Consumers and Certain Producers

According to economic theory, a society's economic well-being is usually measured not by how much it can produce, but how much it can consume. An undervalued RMB that lowers the price of imports from China allows the United States to increase its consumption through an improvement in the terms-of-trade. Since changes in aggregate spending are only temporary, from a long-term perspective, the lasting effect of an undervalued RMB is to increase the purchasing power of U.S. consumers. Imports from China are not limited to consumption goods. U.S. firms also import capital equipment and inputs from China to produce finished goods. An undervalued RMB lowers the price of these U.S. products, increasing their output, and thus making such firms more internationally competitive. An appreciation of China's currency could raise prices for U.S. consumers, lowering their economic welfare, meaning they have less money to spend on other goods and services. In addition, firms that use imported Chinese parts could face higher costs, making them relatively less competitive.

Effect on U.S. Borrowers

An undervalued RMB also has an effect on U.S. borrowers. When the United States runs a current account deficit with China, an equivalent amount of capital flows from China to the United States, as can be seen in the U.S. balance of payments accounts. This occurs because the Chinese central bank or private Chinese citizens are investing in U.S. assets, which allows more U.S. capital investment in plant and equipment to take place than would otherwise occur. Capital investment increases because the greater demand for U.S. assets puts downward pressure on U.S. interest rates, and firms are now willing to make investments that were previously unprofitable. This increases aggregate spending in the short run, all else equal, and also increases the size of the economy in the long run by increasing the capital stock. The effect on interest rates is likely to be greater during periods of robust economic growth, when investment demand is strong, than when the economy is weak.

Private firms are not the only beneficiaries of the lower interest rates caused by the capital inflow (trade deficit) from China. Interest-sensitive household spending, on goods such as consumer durables and housing, is also higher than it would be if capital from China did not flow into the United States. In addition, a large proportion of the U.S. assets bought by the Chinese, particularly by the central bank, are U.S. Treasury securities, which fund U.S. federal budget deficits. According to the U.S. Treasury Department, China held about $1.3 trillion in U.S. Treasury securities as of May 2013, making it the largest foreign holder of such securities.

The U.S. federal budget deficit increased sharply in FY2008 and FY2009, causing a sharp increase in the amount of Treasury securities that had to be sold. During this period, while the Obama Administration pushed China to appreciate its currency, it also encouraged China to continue to purchase U.S. securities, which China did.[86]

Some analysts contend that, although an appreciation of China's currency could help boost U.S. exports to China, it could also lessen China's need to buy U.S. Treasury securities, which could push up U.S. interest rates. In the unlikely worst case scenario, if China stopped buying Treasury securities at a time when the U.S. budget deficit is unusually high, it could make private investors reevaluate their views on the sustainability of current fiscal policy.[87]

Net Effect on the U.S. Economy

In the medium run, according to economic theory, an undervalued RMB neither increases nor decreases aggregate demand in the United States. Rather, it leads to a compositional shift in U.S. production, away from U.S. exporters and import-competing firms toward the firms that benefit from Chinese capital flows. Thus, it might be expected to have no medium- or long-run effect on aggregate U.S. employment or unemployment. As evidence, one can consider that since the 1980s, the U.S. trade deficit has tended to rise when unemployment was falling (and the economy was growing) and fall when unemployment was rising (and the economy was slowing). For example, the U.S. current account deficit peaked at 6.0% of GDP in 2006, when the unemployment rate was 4.6%, and fell to 2.7% of GDP in 2009, when the unemployment rate was 9.3%.

However, the gains and losses in employment and production caused by the trade deficit will not be dispersed evenly across regions and sectors of the economy: on balance, some areas will gain while others will lose. And by shifting the composition of U.S. output to a higher capital base, the size of the economy would be larger in the long run as a result of the capital inflow/trade deficit (although the returns from foreign-financed capital wpuld not flow to Americans).

Although the compositional shift in output has no negative effect on aggregate U.S. output and employment in the long run, there may be adverse short-run consequences. If U.S. output in the trade sector falls more quickly than the increases in output of U.S. recipients of Chinese capital, aggregate U.S. spending and employment could temporarily fall. This is more likely to be a concern if the economy is already sluggish than if it is at full employment. Otherwise, it is likely that government macroeconomic policy adjustment and market forces can compensate for any decline of output in the trade sector by expanding other elements of aggregate demand. The U.S. trade deficit with China (or with the world as a whole) has not prevented the U.S. economy from registering high rates of growth in the past.

A Yale University study estimated that a 25% appreciation of the RMB would initially decrease U.S. imports from China and lead to greater domestic production in the United States and increased exports to China. However, the study estimated that benefits to the U.S. economy would be offset by lower Chinese economic growth (because of falling exports), which would diminish its demand for imports, including those from the United States. In addition, the RMB appreciation would increase U.S. costs for imported products from China (decreasing real wealth and real wages), and cause higher U.S. short-term interest rates. As a result, the sum effect of the 25% RMB appreciation was estimated to a negative effect on U.S. aggregate demand and output and result in a loss of 57,100 U.S. jobs—less than one-tenth of 1% of total U.S. employment.[88]

Analysis by the IMF suggests that currency appreciation alone by China would yield limited benefits to the global economy (including the U.S. economy) unless it was accompanied by greater Chinese consumption and an expansion of the services sector. It estimated that a 20% RMB appreciation would boost U.S. economic growth by 0.05% to 0.07%, while a 20% RMB appreciation plus other reforms for rebalancing the Chinese economy would boost U.S. growth by over 0.15%.[89] The same study also estimated that a 20% RMB appreciation alone could reduce Chinese economic growth by a range of 2.0% to 8.8%, while combining RMB appreciation with reforms for rebalancing could have a range of outcomes from boosting growth by 1% to reducing it by 2%.

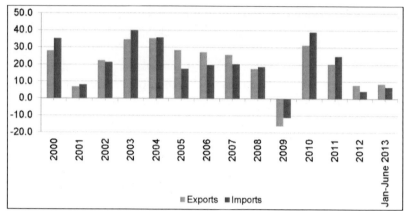

Source: Global Trade Atlas using official Chinese statistics.
Note. Data for 2000-2012 are annual changes. Data for January-June 2013 are year-on-year changes.

Figure 10. Change in China's Trade Flows: 2000-June 2013 (%).

CHINA'S PERSPECTIVE AND CONCERNS: ECONOMIC GROWTH AND STABILITY

Chinese officials argue that their currency policy is not meant to favor exports over imports, but instead to foster economic stability through currency stability. The policy reflects the government's goals of using exports as a way of providing jobs to Chinese workers and to attract FDI in order to gain access to technology and know-how. The Chinese government has stated on a number of occasions that currency reform is a long-term goal which will be implemented gradually. Officials have strongly condemned international pressure to induce China to appreciate the currency, arguing that it interferes with China's "sovereignty" to implement its own domestic economic policies. In 2009, (then) Chinese Premier Wen Jiabao was reported by Chinese media as complaining that "some countries demand the yuan's appreciation, while practicing various trade protectionism against China. It's unfair and actually limits China's development."

Despite the Chinese government's numerous pledges on currency reform, it has moved somewhat cautiously. Chinese officials view economic growth as critical to sustaining political stability, and thus appear very reluctant to implement policies that might disrupt the economy and cause widespread unemployment, which could cause worker unrest.[90] In addition, Chinese officials reject assertions by some economists that China's currency policy undermines the global economy or that a sharp appreciation of the RMB is needed to boost global economic recovery. Instead, they contend, promoting rapid domestic growth is the most significant policy China can undertake to promote global economic recovery. They note that Chinese imports rose by 38.8% in 2010 (over the previous year) and by 23.9% in 2011, which contributed to global economic recovery in those years. They further note that export growth in 2012 and the first half of 2013 was significantly below historic rates (see **Figure 10**).[91] In addition, they note, China's merchandise trade surplus fell each year from 2009 to 2011. In June 2013, Xinhua claimed that the yuan was nearing equilibrium against the dollar.[92]

The Effects of an Undervalued RMB on China's Economy

If the RMB is undervalued vis-à-vis the dollar, then Chinese exports to the United States are likely less expensive than they would be if the currency were freely traded, providing a boost to China's export industries. Eliminating exchange rate risk through a managed peg also increases the attractiveness of China as a destination for foreign investment in export-oriented production facilities. However, there are a number of potentially negative aspects to China's export growth strategy and currency policy.

- Overdependence on exporting (and fixed investment relating to exports) and FDI inflows made China particularly vulnerable to the effects of the global economic slowdown. Analysis by the IMF estimated that fixed investment related to tradable goods plus net exports together accounted for over 60% of China's GDP growth from 2001 to 2008 (up from 40% from 1990 to 2000), which was significantly higher than in the G-7 countries (16%), the euro area (30%) and the rest of Asia (35%).[93]
- An undervalued currency makes imports more expensive, hurting Chinese firms that import parts, machinery, and raw materials. Such a policy, in effect, benefits Chinese exporting firms (many of which are owned by foreign multinational corporations) at the expense of non-exporting Chinese firms. This may impede the most efficient allocation of resources in the Chinese economy. Resources that might

go to other sectors, such as the service sector, are diverted to the export sector.

- If one considers an undervalued currency as a form of export subsidy, then China, in effect, is subsidizing American living standards by selling products that are less expensive than they would be under market conditions. This in effect lowers China's terms of trade—the level of imports that can be obtained through exports.[94] Chinese citizens, on the other hand, pay more for tradable goods, not only because imported goods are more expensive because of the de facto tariff an undervalued currency entails, but also because domestic competition is restricted as well. Rather than use its trade surpluses to purchase goods and services from abroad, China is forced, because of its need to maintain its peg to the dollar, to put a large share of its foreign exchange holdings into U.S. debt securities, which earn a relatively low return.

- The use of a pegged system greatly limits the ability of the central government to use monetary policy to control inflation. If Chinese banks raised interest rates in an effort to control inflation, overseas investors might to try to shift funds to China (through illegal means) to take advantage of the higher Chinese rates. The Chinese government has had difficulty blocking such inflows of "hot money." Such inflows force the government to boost the money supply to buy up the foreign currency necessary to maintain the targeted peg. Expanding the money supply contributes to easy credit policies by the banks, which has contributed to overcapacity in a number of sectors, such as steel, and speculative asset bubbles, such as in real estate.[95] In the past, the Chinese government has tried to use administrative controls, with limited results, to limit bank loans to sectors where overcapacity is believed to exist. In effect, a pegged currency induces the Chinese government to utilize inefficient and non-market financial policies for credit allocation, rather than a market-based system that would promote an efficient allocation of capital.

Although a rebalancing of China's economy, including the adoption of a market-based currency, would likely entail significant adjustment costs, it also would likely produce long-term benefits to the Chinese economy. For example, it could:

China's Currency Policy: An Analysis of the Economic Issues   81

- Boost China's term of trade by increasing the level of imports that can be purchased by its exports;
- Increase economic efficiency (and hence economic growth), by re-directing resources away from inefficient (and often subsidized) sectors of the economy to those that are more efficient and competitive;
- Lower prices for imported goods and services and expose more of the domestic economy to greater global competition, thus lowering prices for consumers and improving Chinese living standards;
- Improve the efficiency and competiveness of many Chinese domestic firms (including those that produce only for the domestic market) by lowering prices for imported inputs, raw materials, and machinery, thus boosting their output;
- Expand the ability of the government to use monetary policies to control inflation and to allocate capital according to its most efficient use through a market-based credit system;
- Help alleviate the large disparities of economic development between the coastal regions of China (as well as growing income disparities throughout China) that have been driven in part by China's export growth strategy and are viewed by many analysts as posing a potential risk to stability;
- Reduce or eliminate a major source of tension between China and many of its trading partners, some of whom view China's undervalued currency and its use of subsidies as beggar-thy-neighbor policies that promote economic development in China at the expense of growth in other countries.

The great challenge for Chinese leaders, assuming that they are committed to greater economic reform and rebalancing the economy, would be to quickly generate new sources of economic growth and job opportunities in order to offset the decline of those sectors that would no longer be able to compete once preferential government policies (such as subsidies and an undervalued currency) are eliminated. However, some analysts contend that this rebalancing could prove difficult for China politically and could take several years to achieve. For example, according to Michael Pettis, reforming China's economic policies would have to involve political reforms because "eliminating the mechanisms by which Chinese policymakers can transfer income from households to manufacturers will reduce their control over the commanding heights of the economy, and it will sharply reduce the power and leverage the ruling party has over business and local governments."[96] On the other hand, China's economy has consistently generated annual growth rates near 10% in recent decades, making adjustment much easier.

POLICY OPTIONS FOR THE RMB AND POTENTIAL OUTCOMES

If the Chinese were to allow their currency to float, it would be determined by private actors in the market based on the supply and demand for Chinese goods and assets relative to U.S. goods and assets. If the RMB appreciated as a result, this would boost U.S. exports and the output of U.S. producers who compete with the Chinese. The U.S. bilateral trade deficit would likely decline (but not necessarily disappear). At the same time, the Chinese central bank would no longer purchase U.S. assets to maintain the peg. U.S. borrowers, including the federal government, would now need to find new lenders to finance their borrowing, and interest rates in the United States would rise. This would reduce spending on interest-sensitive purchases, such as capital investment, housing (residential investment), and consumer durables. The reduction in investment spending would reduce the long-run size of the U.S. capital stock, and thereby the U.S. economy. In the present context of a large U.S. budget deficit, some analysts fear that a sudden decline in Chinese demand for U.S. assets (because China was no longer purchasing assets to influence the exchange rate) could lead to a drop in the value of the dollar that could potentially destabilize the U.S. economy.[97]

If the relative demand for Chinese goods and assets were to fall at some point in the future, the floating exchange rate would depreciate, and the effects would be reversed. Floating exchange rates fluctuate in value frequently and significantly.[98]

A move to a floating exchange rate is typically accompanied by the elimination of capital controls that limit a country's private citizens from freely purchasing and selling foreign currency. The Chinese government maintains capital controls (and arguably one of the major reasons China opposes a floating exchange rate) because it fears a large private capital outflow would result if such controls were removed. This might occur because Chinese citizens fear that their deposits in the potentially insolvent state

China's Currency Policy: An Analysis of the Economic Issues   83

banking system are unsafe. If the capital outflow were large enough, a banking crisis in China could result and could cause the floating exchange rate to depreciate rather than appreciate.[99] If this occurred, the output of U.S. exporters and import- competing firms would be reduced below the prevailing level, and the U.S. bilateral trade deficit would likely expand. In other words, the United States would still borrow heavily from China, but it would now be private citizens buying U.S. assets instead of the Chinese central bank. China could attempt to float its exchange rate while maintaining its capital controls, at least temporarily. This solution would eliminate the possibility that the currency would depreciate because of a private capital outflow. While this would be unusual, it might be possible. It would likely make it more difficult to impose effective capital controls, however, since the fluctuating currency would offer a much greater profit incentive for evasion.

Another possibility is for China to maintain the status quo. Even without adjustment to the nominal exchange rate, over time the real rate would adjust as inflation rates in the two countries diverged. The Chinese central bank acquires foreign reserves by printing yuan to finance its trade surplus. As the central bank exchanged newly printed yuan for U.S. assets, prices in China would rise along with the money supply until the real exchange rate was brought back into line with the market rate.[100] This would cause the U.S. bilateral trade deficit to decline and expand the output of U.S. exporters and import-competing firms. This real exchange rate adjustment would only occur over time, however, and pressures on the U.S. trade sector would persist in the meantime.

None of the solutions guarantee that the bilateral trade deficit would be eliminated. China is a country with a high saving rate, and the United States is a country with a low saving rate; it is not surprising that their overall trade balances would be in surplus and deficit, respectively. As the **Appendix** discusses, many economists believe that these trade imbalances will persist as long as underlying macroeconomic imbalances persist. At the bilateral level, it is not unusual for two countries to run persistently imbalanced trade, even with a floating exchange rate. If China can continue its combination of low-cost labor and rapid productivity gains, which have been reducing export prices in yuan terms, its exports to the United States are likely to continue to grow regardless of the exchange rate regime, as evidenced by the 21% appreciation of the RMB from 2005 to 2008, which did not lead to any reduction in the trade deficit over that period.

CONCLUSION

Congressional concerns over China's currency policy date back to at least 2003. Since that time, the RMB has appreciated significantly against the dollar: 34% on a nominal basis and 42% on a real basis through June 2013. China's current account surplus as a percent of GDP, in dollar terms and as a percent of GDP, has sharply declined significantly in recent years. In 2011, the IMF evaluated the RMB to be substantially undervalued, but in 2012 and 2013, the RMB was estimated to be moderately undervalued. These factors appear to have somewhat diminished the importance of China's currency policy as a priority trade issue for some in Congress.[101] In addition, China has become viewed by some Members as one of several countries that are intervening to hold down the value of their currencies. For example, recent Japanese monetary policies to boost the economy have led some Members and U.S. business groups to accuse Japan of manipulating its currency. Finally in recent years, a number of other Chinese economic policies and practices have been identified by some Members as posing significant threats to U.S. economic interests. These include Chinese cyber-enabled theft of U.S. trade secrets and business confidential information, extensive economic losses incurred by U.S. intellectual property- intensive firms from Chinese infringement of U.S. intellectual property rights, and China's widespread use of industrial policies to subsidize priority domestic firms, while imposing trade and investment barriers to limit foreign market access in China.

The lingering effects of the global economic slowdown (especially in Europe and the United States) have suppressed global demand for Chinese products.[102] The World Bank, IMF, and other global economic institutions have warned China that the policies it has employed to promote high levels of gross fixed investment, financed largely by easy credit policies, are not sustainable and may ultimately seriously weaken China's financial sector by significantly increasing the level of non-performing loans. They have urged China to implement policies to make private consumption the main source of China's economic growth and to eliminate policies that prevent markets from determining the most efficient allocation of resources (such as capital) in the economy in order to ensure that healthy economic growth is sustained over the long term. Reform of the financial sector, including the adoption of a market-determined exchange rate system, would likely play a critical role in this process. Chinese officials have acknowledged the need to make such reforms and have announced a number of policies to that end.[103] For example, during the July 2013 S&ED, Chinese officials stated that that they would continue to

China's Currency Policy: An Analysis of the Economic Issues   85

implement policies to boost private consumption, such as raising social security and employment spending by two percentage points of total fiscal spending by the end of 2015. The implementation of comprehensive economic reforms and a rebalancing of the Chinese economy, if achieved, would likely lead to a significant improvement in U.S.-China commercial relations. For example, as long as the Chinese government continues to maintain a managed currency peg, then the RMB would be assumed by many analysts to be undervalued, regardless of current economic conditions. If the RMB were allowed to be traded freely, without intervention by the Chinese government, then the exchange rate of the RMB against the dollar and other currencies would more likely be viewed as being determined by market forces and hence not undervalued.

APPENDIX. INDICATORS OF U.S. AND CHINESE ECONOMIC IMBALANCES

The issue of rebalancing economic growth by both the United States and China has been a central focus of the U.S.-China Strategic and Economic Dialogue (S&ED) talks over the past two years. A joint statement issued at the May 2011 S&ED meeting noted that

> Since the second meeting of the Strategic and Economic Dialogue in May 2010, the economic recoveries in the United States and China have strengthened due to continued forceful stimulus measures undertaken by both countries, contributing to an improving outlook for the global economy. The two countries have also made progress on their commitments to promote more sustainable and balanced growth. To secure these gains and address potential challenges to the global outlook, we pledge to enhance macroeconomic cooperation to ensure that the global recovery is durable and promotes steady job growth, and to firmly establish strong, sustainable, and balanced growth.[104]

The global financial crisis and subsequent GDP decline among many countries have resulted in new scrutiny by many economists of "global imbalances," namely the disparities in savings and investment levels among various countries (i.e., some countries save too little and some too much relative to their investment needs), and subsequent current account imbalances that have resulted (i.e., countries where domestic savings exceed investment run trade surpluses, and countries where domestic investment exceeds saving run current account deficits). China and the United States are not unique in having these imbalances—Japan, Germany, and other East Asian countries are other examples of high savers, while southern and eastern European countries are other examples of high borrowers. Nevertheless, the United States and China have come under particular scrutiny because of their relative overall size (they are the world's two largest economies) and the relative size of their saving, investment, and trade imbalances. Some analysts also claim that China's exchange rate policy is preventing other East Asian countries from adjusting, because those countries are unwilling to allow their currencies to appreciate and lose export market share to China unless the RMB appreciates too.

Many economists contend such imbalances were a major cause of the current global economic slowdown. For example, high savers, such as China, loaned their money to low savers, such as the United States, which helped keep real U.S. interest rates low and contributed to the bubble in the U.S. housing market and subsequent financial crisis. Many of the high savings countries (especially those in Asia) heavily relied on exporting as a source of their economic growth and thus were significantly impacted when global demand for imports sharply fell.[105] As a result, many economists have called for economic restructuring among many of the world's major economies, especially the United States and China. Fundamental restructuring of this sort would take time, and if not well coordinated, could deepen the global output gap in the short run. For example, if low saving countries attempt to increase their saving rate (e.g., by reducing their government budget deficits) at a time of high unemployment, and high saving countries do not simultaneously increase their consumption, then worldwide demand could decline and cause unemployment to rise further in the short run.

This section provides an overview of some of the unique differences between the economies of the United States and China that have played a role in global imbalances and examines if there has been any rebalancing by the U.S. and Chinese economies in recent years.

Current Account Balances, Savings, and Investment

The level of U.S. gross savings is far below total U.S. investment, indicating that the United States must borrow capital abroad to meet its investment needs. By definition, domestic savings minus gross investment (from domestic and foreign sources) equals the current account balance.[106]

China's Currency Policy: An Analysis of the Economic Issues

Nations that do not save enough to meet domestic investment needs run current account deficits and those that save more than they need for domestic investment run current account surpluses.[107] In 2012, the ratio of U.S. gross domestic savings to gross investment was 77.3%, the lowest among the world's major economies. On the other hand, the ratio for China was 105.7% (see **Table A-1**).

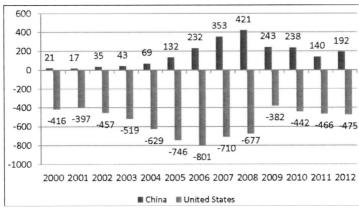

Source: International Monetary Fund.

Figure A-1. Chinese and U.S. Current Account Balances: 2000-2012 ($ billions).

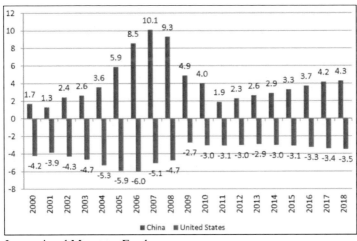

Source: International Monetary Fund.

Figure A-2. Chinese and U.S. Current Account Balances as a Percent of GDP: 2000-2012 and Estimates Through 2018 (percent).

Table A-1. Ratio of Gross National Savings to Gross Investment and Current Account Balances as a Percent of GDP for Selected Major Economies: 2012

	Gross National Savings/Gross Investment (%)	Current Account Balance/GDP (%)
United Kingdom	75.5	-3.5
United States	77.3	-3.0
Canada	84.9	-3.7
India	84.9	-4.8
Brazil	85.7	-2.4
France	88.1	-2.4
Indonesia	92.5	-2.7
Mexico	96.7	-0.8
Japan	104.8	1.0
China	105.7	2.3
Russia	115.7	4.0
South Korea	116.3	4.3
Germany	134.9	6.3

Source: Economist Intelligence Unit and International Monetary Fund.

In nominal dollar terms, the United States had the world's largest current account deficit in 2012 at $475 billion, while China had the largest current account surplus at $192 billion (see **Figure A-1**). These balances were also significant as a share of GDP: -3.0% for the United States and 2.3% for China (see **Figure A-2**).[108] Some "rebalancing" has taken place during and after the global recession. The U.S. current account deficit has declined from its peak 6.0% in 2006 because domestic investment spending has fallen and the private savings has risen.[109] In addition, the U.S. federal budget deficit as a percent of GDP fell from 10.1% in FY2009 to 7.0% in FY2012, and is projected to decline to 4.0% in FY2013, according to the Congressional Budget Office (CBO).[110] What remains to be seen is how much of this rebalancing is cyclical, and will be reversed when the U.S. economy returns to full employment, and how much of it is permanent. The IMF projects China's current account balance as a percent of GDP will increase over the next six years to 4.3% in 2018, but still significantly lower than its historical high of 10.1% in 2007. The U.S. current account deficit as a percent of GDP is projected by the IMF to grow to 3.5% of GDP in 2018, also much lower than its historic peak of 6.0% in 2006.

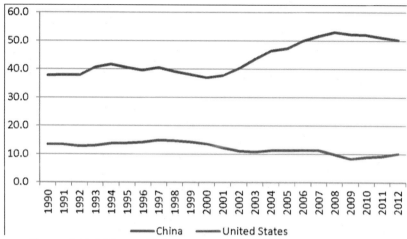

Source: Economist Intelligence Unit.
Notes: Aggregate national savings by the public and private sector as a percentage of nominal GDP.

Figure A-3. Gross National Savings as a Percent of GDP for China and the United States: 1990-2012 (percent).

Despite the rebalancing that has already taken place, some economists would not consider either country to have reached a position that is sustainable in the long run. Before the late 1990s, the United States had never had a current account deficit of 3% of GDP. And even with China's reduced current account surplus and the diminished U.S. current account deficit over the past few years, China's net holdings of foreign assets and the U.S. net foreign debt continue to grow. Likewise, the decline in China's current account surplus was caused by a more rapid decline in China's exports than imports during the worldwide economic downturn—when worldwide growth picks up again and reaches pre-crisis levels, that trend could reverse.

Gross saving is the total level of domestic saving, including private, corporate, and government. Saving represents income that is not consumed. Physical investment spending on plant and equipment can be financed from domestic or foreign saving. Over the past several years, the United States has maintained one of the lowest gross saving rates (i.e., total national saving as a percent of GDP) among developed countries, while China has maintained one of the world's highest national saving rates. From 1990 to 2009, U.S. gross national saving as a percent of GDP declined from 13.5% to 8.4%, while China's rose from 37.8% to 52.3% (see **Figure A-3**). U.S. gross saving as a percent of GDP increased over the next three years, reaching 10.4% in 2012. Chinese gross savings levels have declined over the next three years, reaching 50.4% in 2012.

Chinese Investment and Consumption Relative to GDP

As indicated in **Figure A-4**, China's gross investment as a percent of GDP rose from 25.0% in 1990 to 44.9% in 2009—the highest of any major economy (in comparison, the U.S. rate was 12.2%—the lowest among the major economies). China's investment as a percent of GDP rose to 46.1% in 2012. China's private consumption as a percent of GDP dropped from 48.8% in 1990 to 35.4% in 2009—the lowest among any major economy (while the U.S. rate in 2009 was 70.5%, which was the highest among the major economies). Chinese private consumption as a percent of GDP was 35.7% in 2012.

Although private consumption has been a much smaller share of China's GDP than other countries, the growth rate of China's private consumption has been significant. From 2001 to 2012, Chinese private consumption grew at an average annual rate of 8.4%, which was much faster than the growth in real U.S. private consumption, but slower than the overall growth rate of the Chinese economy (see **Figure A-5**).

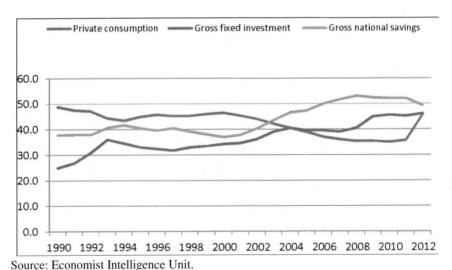

Source: Economist Intelligence Unit.

Figure A-4. Chinese Private Consumption, Investment, and Gross National Savings as a Percent of GDP: 1990-2012.

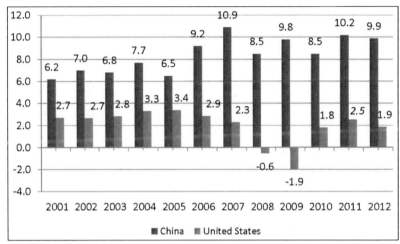

Source: Economist Intelligence Unit.

Figure A-5. Annual Growth in Real Chinese and U.S. Private Consumption: 2001-2012 (percent increase over the previous year).

Many analysts contend that, although Chinese labor productivity has risen rapidly over the past several years, workers' wages have not kept pace with those productivity gains, largely due to the lack of worker rights in China, especially for migrant workers who tend to seek work in labor- intensive, export oriented, manufacturing. Rather, it is argued, the gains from productivity have largely accrued to Chinese firms.[111] In addition, because the Chinese government maintains tight controls on capital outflows, Chinese households are limited in terms of where they can invest their savings. Most choose to deposit their savings in a Chinese bank. However, bank interest rates are set by the central government, and oftentimes, the rates of return on savings deposits are below the rate of inflation (see **Figure A-7**). Chinese depositors faced negative real interest rates in 2004, 2007, 2008, 2010, and 2011. Many economists contend that this policy represents an effort by the central government to keep the cost of credit low for Chinese firms (in order to boost fixed investment), but that this comes at the expense of Chinese households whose savings deposits can actually lose value, thus forcing them to save more of their income to cover the costs of health care, retirement, and other large expenses.

Some have concluded that Chinese controls on bank interest rates have dampened the level of household spending/consumption that would have been expected, given the rapid rate of China's economic growth.[112] As indicated in

Figure A-6, China's personal disposable income as a percent of GDP declined from 56.5% in 2002 to 48.9% in 2009, indicating that Chinese households did not benefit as much from China's economic growth as other sectors of the economy. That rate fell to 48.5% in 2010, but increased to 49.4% in 2011 and to 51.6% in 2012.

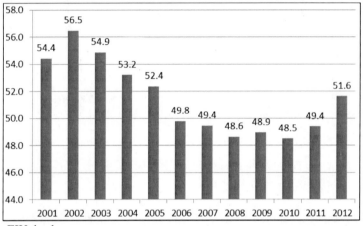

Source: EIU database.

Figure A-6. Chinese Personal Disposal Income as a Percent of GDP: 2001-2012 (%).

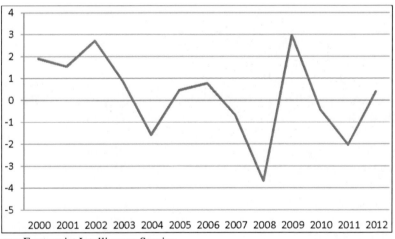

Source: Economist Intelligence Service.
Notes: Interest rates on one-year deposits adjusted for changes in the consumer price index.

Figure A-7. Chinese Real Deposit Interest Rates: 2000-2012 (percent).

China's Currency Policy: An Analysis of the Economic Issues   93

Many economists contend that the goal of rebalancing the Chinese economy toward greater reliance on personal consumption cannot be achieved until the central government eliminates distortive economic policies that favor firms over households. Once such policy relates to the government's control over much of the country's banking system.

Sources of China's Economic Growth

The sources of China's real GDP growth from 2006-2012 are shown in **Figure A-8**. Gross fixed investment (some of which is linked to tradable sectors) was the largest contributor to its real GDP growth over much of this period. The sharp growth in fixed investment in 2009 appears to reflect the results of the Chinese government's $586 billion stimulus package and its monetary easing policy that encouraged banks to expand lending—a significant amount of which is believed to have gone to infrastructure projects. In 2009, changes to net exports in China were a drag on the Chinese economy, while in 2010 they provided a modest contribution to GDP growth. In 2012, private consumption was the largest contributor to China's GDP growth.[113]

The next few years could be a critical period for China's economic policymakers. A number of economists have questioned the quality of China's massive investment efforts over the past two years and the ability of local government to repay the loans they took out to fund major investment projects. Thus, the importance of fixed investment to China's economic growth over the next few years could decline. The Chinese government's 12th Five Year Plan (2011-2015) states that rebalancing the economy, promoting consumer demand, boosting rural incomes, addressing income disparity (such as boosting wages), promoting the development of the services sector, and expanding social welfare programs (such as education, social security, and health care) will be major priorities. Such policies, if implemented, could provide a significant boost to consumer spending. Based on China's historical economic model, it will likely take several years for a significant rebalancing of the Chinese economy to occur. In addition, many economists have raised concerns that, as China's major trading partners, such as the United States and Europe, begin to experience more rapid economic growth, their demand for Chinese products will increase, which could discourage China's government from following through on economic reforms necessary to promote a rebalancing of the economy.

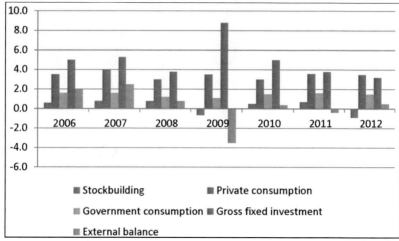

Source: Economist Intelligence Unit.

Figure A-8. Chinese Real GDP Growth and Sources of GDP Growth: 2006-2012 (percentage points).

End Notes

[1] The official name of China's currency is the renminbi (RMB), which is denominated in yuan units. Both RMB and yuan are used interchangeably to describe China's currency.

[2] The White House, *Remarks by the President at the Senate Democratic Policy Committee Issues Conference*, February 3, 2010.

[3] The White House, *News Conference by President Obama*, November 14, 2011.

[4] These were government-sanctioned foreign exchange adjustment centers (established in 1986) to allow a limited amount of trade in foreign exchange, although the central government intervened to prevent the RMB from strengthening beyond 6 yuan per dollar. Source: U.S. Department of State, *Country Reports on Economic Policy and Trade Practices*, February 1990, p. 253.

[5] Overseas investment by Chinese citizens is tightly regulated and restricted by the central government. For example, it would be very difficult for a Chinese citizen to open a savings account in another country or invest in shares of foreign stocks without permission from the government. Limiting capital outflows from China is a key policy tool of the central government to control exchange rates within China. In addition, some analysts contend that China fears that an open capital account would lead to capital flight, which could undermine its financial system.

[6] It was later announced that the composition of the basket would include the dollar, the yen, the euro, and a few other currencies, although the currency composition of the basket has never been revealed. If the value of the yuan were determined according to a basket of currencies, however, it would not have shown the stability it has had against the dollar between mid-2008 and mid-2010, unless the basket were overwhelmingly weighted toward dollars.

[7] China Daily, February 3, 2009, at http://www.chinadaily.com.cn/china/2009-02/03/content_7440106.htm.

China's Currency Policy: An Analysis of the Economic Issues   95

[8] The fact that the currency has appreciated some days but has depreciated on others raises a number of questions as to the extent and pace the PBC will allow the RMB to appreciate over time. Many observers believe that this is a sign that appreciation of the RMB will happen over a long period of time, but in an unpredictable way in an effort to limit RMB speculation and inflows of "hot money," which could destabilize China's economy.

[9] The exchange rate went from 6.30 yuan per dollar to 6.17.

[10] This report uses the monthly consumer price index from Global Insight to calculate the real yuan/dollar exchange rate.

[11] A trade-weighted index reflects the relative importance of each partner's trade with China. The index itself is calculated as the geometric weighted averages of bilateral exchange rates. According to Chinese data, the United States is second largest trading partner after the European Union (EU). Thus the dollar accounts for a significant portion of the index—it averaged 19 points (out of 100) from 2008 to 2010, while the euro averaged 19.4 points.

[12] Bank of International Settlements, BIS Effective Exchange Rates, at http://www.bis.org/ statistics

[13] In comparison, the nominal percentage change in the yuan/dollar exchange rate over these periods was 9.6% and 1.3% (based on monthly averages).

[14] In general, U.S.-invested firms in China do not appear to be as concerned over the value of China's currency relative to the dollar as are U.S. import-sensitive firms that compete with low-priced Chinese products.

[15] China emerged as the world's largest merchandise exporter in 2010 (accounting for 10.1% of global exports) and the seconding largest economy. These rankings have stayed constant through 2012.

[16] The current account balance is the broadest measurement of trade flows because it includes trade in goods and services. It also includes income flows and current transfer payments.

[17] Gagnon, Joseph, *The Elephant Hiding in the Room: Currency Intervention and Trade Imbalances*, Peterson Institute for International Economics, Working Paper 13-2, March 2013, at http://www.piie.com/publications/wp/wp13-2.pdf.

[18] China's accumulation of foreign exchange reserves in the first quarter of 2013 was 3.9% higher than in the previous quarter.

[19] Similarly, China's merchandise trade surplus rose from $32 billion in 2004 to a historical high of $297 billion in 2008. China's merchandise trade surplus declined over the next few years, hitting $158 billion in 2011; it rose to $233 billion in 2012.

[20] IMF, *Press Release*, July 17, 2013, at http://www.imf.org/external/np/sec/pr/2013/ pr13260. htm. Note, the IMF's July 2013 estimates of China's current account surpluses as a percent of GDP in 2011 and 2012 were different than the estimates it made in April 2013 (at 2.8% and 2.6%, respectively).

[21] For additional information on China's response to the global economic crisis, see CRS Report RL33534, *China's Economic Rise: History, Trends, Challenges, and Implications for the United States*, by Wayne M. Morrison.

[22] IMF, *People's Republic of China: 2010 Article IV Consultation—Staff Report; Staff Statement; Public Information Notice on the Executive Board Discussion*, July 2010, p. 1.

[23] IMF, *People's Republic of China: 2010 Article IV Consultation— Staff Report For the 2012 Article IV Consultation*, July 6, 2011, p. 1.

[24] Peterson Institute for International Economics, *Currency Manipulation, the US Economy, and the Global Economic Order*, by C. Fred Bergsten and Joseph E. Gagnon, December 2012.

[25] Other "manipulators" included Japan, Libya, Algeria, Saudi Arabia, Thailand, Malaysia, Israel, South Korea, Argentina, Bolivia, the Philippines, Angola, Kazakhstan, Azerbaijan, Angola, and Russia.

[26] Wall St. Journal, "China Fund Warns Japan Against a 'Currency War,'" March 6, 2013.

[27] *Inside U.S. Trade*, April 13, 2013.

[28] Office of Congressman Sandy Levin, Press Release, "U.S. Announcement on Japan and TPP," April 12, 2013.

[29] Peterson Institute for International Economics, Press Release, May 16, 2013, at http://www.iie.com/publications/newsreleases/newsrelease.cfm?id=203.

[30] Office of Congressman Mike Michaud, Press Release, "Majority of House Members Push Obama to Address Currency Manipulation in TPP," June 6, 2013, at http://michaud.house.gov/press-release/majority-house-members-push-obama-address-currency-manipulation-tpp.

[31] Economic Policy Institute, *the China Toll: Growing U.S. trade deficit with China Cost More Than 2.7 Million Jobs between 2001 and 2011, With Job Losses in Every State*, by Robert E. Scott, August 23, 2012. Note, some have criticized the methodology used in the report, which assumes that the U.S. trade deficit with China has a direct and significant effect on the level of employment in the United States.

[32] Ibid., p. 8.

[33] New York Times, December 31, 2009. Krugman also estimated that China's currency policy caused 1.4 million job losses in the United States.

[34] As required under §3004 of Omnibus Trade and Competitiveness Act of 1988 (22 U.S.C. 5305).

[35] This language appears to have been taken from Article IV, §1 (iii) of the Articles of Agreement of the International Monetary Fund (IMF), which states that members should, among other things "avoid manipulating exchange rates or the international monetary system in order to prevent effective balance of payments adjustment or to gain an unfair competitive advantage over other members."

[36] Many members sharply criticized the Department of the Treasury's decision in April 2010 to delay issuing its first 2010 exchange rate report (usually issued in March or April). That report was issued on July 8, 2010 (after China made its announcement on currency reform), and it did not cite China (or any other country) for currency manipulation.

[37] U.S. Department of Treasury, *Semiannual Report on International Economic and Exchange Rate Policies, Appendix: Analysis of Exchange Rates Pursuant to the Act*, November 2005.

[38] Testimony by C. Fred Bergsten, Peterson Institute of International Economics, *Correcting the Chinese Exchange Rate: an Action Plan*, before the House Ways & Means Committee, March 24, 2010.

[39] Of particular concern to some groups are proposals that would require the U.S. government to calculate the percentage level of a currency's misalignment or undervaluation, since there is no universally-accepted method of making such estimates (see discussion of this issue on page 15). A September, 22, 2011, letter sent by a group of U.S. business organizations to Senators Reid and McConnell argued that any legislation that requires the Commerce Department to estimate the "true" exchange rate would "create a process that will be highly subjective and potentially politicized." A copy of the letter can be found at http://businessroundtable.org/news-center/business-groups-letter-opposing-china-currency-legislation.

[40] A number of U.S. countervailing duty petitions have included claims that China's currency policy is an actionable subsidy under U.S. countervailing duty law. Some petitioners have argued that when Chinese exporters are paid in dollars and subsequently exchange those dollars for Chinese RMB, the payment (RMB) they receive is larger than would occur under market conditions because of the Chinese government's intervention to keep the RMB artificially low against dollar. This policy is viewed as constituting a financial contribution or price support. The Commerce Department has yet to include an undervalued currency as part of its countervailing duty investigation. In one case involving imported aluminum extrusions from China, which included a charge by petitioners that China's undervalued currency was a countervailable subsidy, the Commerce Department stated that additional study of the issue was needed, given the unique nature of the alleged subsidy and the complex methodological issues that it raises under U.S. countervailing duty law. See for example, Department of Commerce, International Trade Administration, *Aluminum*

China's Currency Policy: An Analysis of the Economic Issues   97

Extrusions from the People's Republic of China: Initiation of Countervailing Duty Investigation, Federal Register, Volume 75, Number 80, April 27, 2010, p. 22117.

[41] The benefit would be defined as the difference between the amount of foreign currency received by the exporter from the transaction and the amount that would have been received if the currency was not undervalued.

[42] In other words, the undervalued currency could be considered to be a measure that is contingent upon export performance.

[43] Real effective exchange rates are defined as a weighted average of bilateral exchange rates, adjusted for inflation.

[44] See §3004 of Omnibus Trade and Competitiveness Act of 1988 (22 U.S.C. 5305).

[45] Under U.S. antidumping proceedings regarding imports from a non-market economy country (such as China), the Commerce Department may determine that the normal value of the product in question cannot be determined. In such cases, Commerce uses price information from "surrogate countries" that have a market economy to determine the normal value of the imported products in question. Some analysts contend that this practice results in higher antidumping rates on imports from nonmarket economy countries than on those from market economy countries.

[46] IMF, *Challenges to the International Monetary System: Rebalancing Currencies, Institutions, and Rates, Presentation by Mr. Takatoshi Kato*, September 30, 2011.

[47] The White House, *Remarks by the President at the Senate Democratic Policy Committee Issues Conference*, February 3, 2010.

[48] The White House, *News Conference by President Obama*, November 14, 2011.

[49] The White House, *Press Briefing by Press Secretary Jay Carney*, October 12, 2011.

[50] China's currency issue was also a major topic under the U.S.-China Strategic Economic Dialogue (SED) that was started under the Bush Administration in 2006.

[51] U.S. Department of State, *Joint Closing Remarks for the Strategic and Economic Dialogue*, May 10, 2011, available at http://www.state

[52] Department of the Treasury, Press Release, May 4, 2012, at http://www.treasury.gov/press-center/press- releases/Pages/tg1566.aspx.

[53] The multilateral approach may also act as an inducement for China to reform its currency policies. If other economies (especially Asia) agree not to intervene in currency markets to prevent their currencies from appreciating (or depreciate them to gain a competitive edge against Chinese exporters), China might agree to quicken the pace of currency appreciation and reform. If China went ahead and appreciated its currency, other Asian economies might do the same. This might help minimize Chinese concerns that an appreciating currency would disrupt its export sector.

[54] Department of Treasury, *Dear G-20 Colleagues Letter*, October 20, 2010.

[55] Statement by G7 Finance Ministers and Central Bank Governors, February 12, 2013, at http://www.g8.utoronto.ca/finance/fm130212.htm.

[56] This is often referred to as the real or equilibrium exchange rate and is broadly based on assumptions of what exchange rates would be predicted to be in order to be consistent with a country's fundamental macroeconomic conditions.

[57] Reisen, Helmut, *On the Renminbi and Economic Convergence*, December 17, 2009, available at http://www.voxeu.org/index.php?q=node/4397.

[58] Rodrick, Dani, *Making Room for China in the World Economic*, December 17, 2009, available at http://www.voxeu.org/index.php?q=node/4399.

[59] Cline, William R. and John Williamson, 2009 Estimates of Fundamental Equilibrium Exchange Rates, Peterson Institute for International Economics, Policy Brief PB09-10-2, June 2009, available athttp://www.iie.com/publications/pb/pb09-10.pdf.

[60] Harvard Business School, T*he End of Chimarica*, by Niall Ferguson and Moritz Schularick, Working Paper 10-937, October 2009, available at http://www.hbs.edu/research/pdf/10-037.pdf.

[61] U.S. Treasury Department, *Report on International Economic and Exchange Rate Policies*, December 2006, Appendix II.

[62] The ERER approach estimates an equilibrium real exchange rate for each country as a function of medium-term fundamentals, such as the net foreign asset (NFA) position of the country, relative productivity differential between the tradable and non-tradable sectors, and the terms of trade. The ES approach calculates the difference between the actual current account balance and the balance that would stabilize the NFA position of the country at some benchmark level. The MB approach calculates the difference between the current account balance projected over the medium term at prevailing exchange rates and an estimated equilibrium current account balance, or "CA norm." See International Monetary Fund, *Methodology for CGER Exchange Rate Assessments*, November 8, 2006.

[63] International Monetary Fund, *People's Republic of China, 2011 Article IV Consultation,* July 2011, p.18.

[64] International Monetary Fund, *Methodology for CGER Exchange Rate Assessments*, November 8, 2006, pp. 4-5.

[65] http://www.imf.org/external/pubs/ft/scr/2012/cr12195.pdf

[66] IMF, *Pilot External Sector Report*, July 2, 2012, at http://www.imf.org/external/np/pp/eng/2012/070212.pdf.

[67] IMF, *Transcript of IMF Press Conference at the Conclusion of the 2013 Article IV Consultation Discussions with China,* May 29, 2013.

[68] The semi-annual series of estimates of FEERs was coauthored with John Williamson until his retirement at the end of 2012.

[69] Cline estimates found several currencies to be overvalued as well.

[70] *Correcting the Chinese Exchange Rate: An Action Plan,* by C. Fred Bergsten, Peterson Institute for International Economics, Testimony before the Committee on Ways and Means, U.S. House of Representatives, March 24, 2010.

[71] Some analysts contend that U.S. imports from China grew rapidly from 2001-2004, and slowed from 2005 to 2008, not because of the appreciation of the RMB, but because of changes to U.S. consumer demand relating to macroeconomic conditions.

[72] Trade varied from year to year. In 2008, U.S. imports from China rose by 5.1% over the previous year, compared to import growth of 11.7% in 2007; however, U.S. exports over this period were up 9.5% in 2008 compared with an 18.1% rise in 2007.

[73] The current global economic slowdown led to a sharp reduction in U.S.-China trade in 2009; both U.S. exports to and imports from China fell sharply, though imports fell at a bigger rate. As a result, the U.S. trade deficit with China was down 14.8% over the previous year.

[74] Depending on the elasticity of demand for the product, some might be willing to pay the extra price and buy the same level as before, some might buy less of the product, and some might stop purchasing the product altogether.

[75] Bureau of Labor Statistics, *Import/Export Price Indexes*, Press Release, various issues.

[76] The disparity between changes in the RMB/dollar exchange rate and the changes in import prices of Chinese products is even more pronounced when changes to the exchange rate are adjusted for inflation. Some of the costs may have been borne by Chinese producers or workers. Alternatively, China might have been able to boost efficiency, thus lowering costs, or production could have moved inland where labor is less expensive.

[77] Communications of the ACM, *Who Captures Value in a Global Innovation Network? The Case of Apple's iPod*, March 2009.

[78] He also argues that reducing the federal budget deficit in the long run is the best way to boost employment and states that "in comparative importance, the value of the RMB is a footnote."

[79] Heritage Foundation, WebMemo, *Deadlines and Delays: Chinese Revaluation Will Still Not Bring American Jobs*, April 6, 2010.

[80] Carnegie Endowment for International Peace, *How Can China Reduce Its Reliance on Net Exports?*, June 24, 2010.

China's Currency Policy: An Analysis of the Economic Issues 99

[81] The Federal Reserve Bank of San Francisco Economic Letter, *The U.S. Content of "Made in China,"* August 8, 2011, at http://www.frbsf.org/publications/economics

[82] According to the U.S. Bureau of Economic Analysis, personal consumption expenditures is the primary measure of consumer spending on goods and services in the U.S. economy, accounting for about two-thirds of domestic final spending, and thus it is the primary engine that drives future economic growth. See U.S. Bureau of Economic Analysis website at http://www.bea.gov/national/pdf/NIPAhandbookch5.pdf.

[83] The standard economic model for determining whether countries should have a floating exchange rate is the "optimal currency area" model. According to this model, two countries can gain from fixed exchange rates if their goods and labor markets are highly interconnected and their business cycles are closely synchronized. By these criteria, China and the United States are unlikely to form an optimal currency area.

[84] Many such firms contend that China's currency policy constitutes one of several unfair trade advantages enjoyed by Chinese firms, including low wages, lack of enforcement of safety and environmental standards, selling below cost (dumping) and direct assistance from the Chinese government.

[85] U.S. employment in manufacturing as a share of total non-agricultural employment fell from 31.8% in 1960, to 22.4% in 1980, to 13.1% in 2000, to 8.9% in 2010. This trend is much larger than the Chinese currency issue and is caused by numerous other factors, including productivity gains in manufacturing (such as through new technologies) and the rise of employment in the service sector.

[86] From 2008 to 2010, China's holdings of U.S. Treasury securities increased by $673 billion. However from 2010 to May 2013, China increased its holdings by only $156 billion.

[87] China has expressed concern in recent years over the "safety" of its large holdings of U.S. debt. It has criticized the U.S. Federal Reserve's easy monetary policies to boost economic growth, such as quantitative easing (involving large- scale purchases of U.S. Treasury Securities). Chinese officials claim that such policies could lead to a sharp devaluation of the dollar against global currencies and boost U.S. inflation, which could diminish the value of China's dollar holdings.

[88] Fair, Ray C., "Estimated Macroeconomic Effects Of A Chinese Yuan Appreciation," Cowles Foundation Discussion Paper 1755, March 2010.

[89] International Monetary Fund, *People's Republic of China, 2011 Article IV Consultation,* July 2011, p. 36.

[90] There have been numerous reports of labor unrest and strikes in different parts of China in 2010, mainly over pay issues. Chinese officials are concerned that an appreciation of the RMB could induce Chinese export producers to try to hold down wages to remain competitive, or could force them out of business, which could lead to more job losses and provoke more unrest.

[91] Some recent media reports indicate that data on the level of Chinese exports in 2013 may be overstated because some entities in China may be filing fake export invoices in order to transfer capital to China.

[92] Xinhua News Agency, June 7, 2013, at http://news.xinhuanet.com/english/indepth/2013-06/07/c_124830356.htm.

[93] Guo, Kai and Papa N'Diaye, *Is China's Export-Oriented Growth Sustainable,* IMF Working Paper, August 2009.

[94] The ultimate goal of trade is to obtain imports in exchange for exports. The more imports a country can obtain from a given level of exports, the better off it is materially. China appears to be willing to "subsidize' its exports in order to boost jobs in export-oriented industries. However, Chinese consumers are made worse off.

[95] The government can and has attempted to sterilize the increase of the money supply by forcing state banks to buy and hold government bonds.

[96] Pettis, Michael, *Sharing the Pain: The Global Struggle Over Savings,* Carnegie Endowment for International Peace, November 2009, p. 7.

[97] For more information, see CRS Report R40770, *The Sustainability of the Federal Budget Deficit: Market Confidence and Economic Effects*, by Marc Labonte.

[98] Some economists argue that short-term movements in floating exchange rates cannot always be explained by economic fundamentals. If this were the case, then the floating exchange rate could become inexplicably overvalued (undervalued) at times, reducing (increasing) the output of U.S. exporters and U.S. firms that compete with Chinese imports. These economists often favor fixed or managed exchange rates to prevent these unexplainable fluctuations, which they argue are detrimental to U.S. economic well-being. Other economists argue that movements in floating exchange rates are rational, and therefore lead to economically efficient outcomes. They doubt that governments are better equipped to identify currency imbalances than market professionals.

[99] This argument is made in Morris Goldstein and Nicholas Lardy, "A Modest Proposal for China's Renminbi," *Financial Times*, August 26, 2003. Alternatively, if Chinese citizens proved unconcerned about keeping their wealth in Chinese assets, the removal of capital controls could lead to a greater inflow of foreign capital since foreigners would be less concerned about being unable to access their Chinese investments. This would cause the exchange rate to appreciate.

[100] To some extent, China can reduce the effects of the accumulation of foreign reserves on the money supply through credit controls, although this is unlikely to be completely effective.

[101] Others in Congress, however, continue to view the large and growing U.S. trade deficit with China, and the loss of U.S. manufacturing jobs, to be largely caused by China's currency manipulation.

[102] From January-May 2013, U.S. imports from China were up by only 3.1% year-on-year.

[103] See CRS Report RL33534, *China's Economic Rise: History, Trends, Challenges, and Implications for the United States*, by Wayne M. Morrison.

[104] U.S. Department of the Treasury press release, Third Meeting of the U.S.-China Strategic & Economic Dialogue Joint U.S.-China Economic Track Fact Sheet, May 10, 2011. Available at http://www.treasury.gov/press-center/press- releases/Pages/tg1170.aspx.

[105] For an overview of this argument, see Blanchard, Olivier and Gian Maria Milesi-Ferretti, "Global Imbalances: In Midstream?" IMF Staff Position Note, December 22, 2009.

[106] The current account balance is the broadest measurement of a country's financial flows. It includes the balances for trade in goods and services, net income (investment income and compensation for overseas workers), and net unilateral transfers.

[107] A current account deficit also reflects that a country consumes more than it produces, while a current account surplus indicates that a country produces more than it consumes.

[108] The U.S. current account deficit as a percent of GDP fell in 2008 and 2009. China's current account surplus as a percent of GDP fell each year from 2007 to 2009.

[109] Gross private savings as a percent of GDP rose from 14.2% in 2007 to 18.2% in 2010. Source: Bureau of Economic Analysis.

[110] CBO, *Updated Budget Projections: Fiscal Years 2013 to 2023*, May 14, 2013, at http://www.cbo.gov/publication/44172.

[111] This is not to say that Chinese wages have not gone up in recent years. From 2003 to 2012, real wages increased by 153% or an average annual increase of 11%. Source: EIU.

[112] Chinese house consumption is also repressed because of the lack of an adequate social safety net. This forces them to maintain a high rate of savings in order to pay for medical costs, education, and future retirement costs (if they don't have a pension).

[113] The last time this occurred was 2000.

In: Exchange Rates and Currency Debates
Editor: Darren Byers

ISBN: 978-1-62948-616-1
© 2013 Nova Science Publishers, Inc.

Chapter 3

THE DEPRECIATING DOLLAR: ECONOMIC EFFECTS AND POLICY RESPONSE[*]

Craig K. Elwell

SUMMARY

A trend depreciation of the dollar since 2002 raises concern among some in Congress and the public that the dollar's decline is a symptom of broader economic problems, such as a weak economic recovery, rising public debt, and a diminished standing in the global economy. However, a falling currency is not always a problem, but possibly an element of economic adjustments that are, on balance, beneficial to the economy.

A depreciating currency could affect several aspects of U.S. economic performance. Possible effects include increased net exports, decreased international purchasing power, rising commodity prices, and upward pressure on interest rates; if the trend is sustained, the United states may also experience a reduction of external debt, possible undermining of the dollar's reserve currency status, and an elevated risk of a dollar crisis.

The exchange rate is not a variable that is easily addressed by changes in legislative policy. Nevertheless, although usually not the primary target, the dollar's international value can be affected by decisions made on policy issues facing the 112th Congress, including

---

[*] This is an edited, reformatted and augmented version of a Congressional Research Service publication, CRS Report for Congress RL34582, prepared for Members and Committees of Congress, from www.crs.gov, dated February 23, 2012.

decisions related to generating jobs, raising the debt limit, reducing the budget deficit, and stabilizing the growth of the federal government's long-term debt. Also monetary policy actions by the Federal Reserve, over which Congress has oversight responsibilities, can affect the dollar.

The exchange rate of the dollar is largely determined by the market—the supply and demand for dollars in global foreign exchange markets associated with the buying and selling of dollar denominated goods, services, and assets (e.g., stocks, bonds, real property) on global markets. In most circumstances, however, international asset-market transactions will tend to be dominant, with the size and strength of inflows and outflows of capital ultimately determining whether the exchange rate appreciates or depreciates.

A variety of factors can influence the size and direction of cross-border asset flows. Of principal importance are the likely rate of return on the asset, investor expectations about a currency's future path, the size and liquidity of the country's asset markets, the need for currency diversification in international investors' portfolios, changes in the official holdings of foreign exchange reserves by central banks, and the need for and location of investment safe havens. All of these factors could themselves be influenced by economic policy choices.

To give Congress the economic context in which to view the dollar's recent and prospective movement, this report analyzes the evolution of the exchange rate since its peak in 2002. It examines several factors that are likely to influence the dollar's medium-term path, what effects a depreciating dollar could have on the economy, and how alternative policy measures that could be taken by the Federal Reserve, the Treasury, and the 112th Congress might influence the dollar's path.

INTRODUCTION

From a peak in early 2002 through the first half of 2008, the (inflation adjusted) trade-weighted dollar exchange rate, for the most part, steadily depreciated, falling a total of about 25% (see *Figure 1*). The dollar's fall over this six-year period was moderately paced at about 3% to 4% annually. For the next nine months, as the wider economy was reeling from the effects of the financial crisis and recession, the dollar sharply appreciated, increasing more than 11% on a trade-weighted basis.[1] For reasons that will be discussed later in the report, this appreciation was a market response to the great uncertainty associated with those economic troubles. As economic conditions began to stabilize in mid-2009, the dollar began to depreciate again and fell about 16% through mid-2011 and more or less returned to its prerecession trend of

The Depreciating Dollar: Economic Effects and Policy Response   103

depreciation. However, a second bout of market uncertainty caused by the European sovereign debt crisis caused the dollar to appreciate more than 5% through the end of 2011. In early 2012, the dollar resumed its depreciation, down about 2% through February 2012 and, with the return of some degree of financial normalcy in Europe, the trend depreciation some believe may resume.

The dollar's fall from early 2002 through early 2008 as well as the recent depreciation has not been uniform against individual currencies, however. For example, in the earlier period, it fell 45% against the euro, 24% against the yen, 18% against the yuan, and 17% against the Mexican peso. In the period since the trough of the business cycle in mid-2009, the dollar fell 13% against the euro, 11% against the yen, less than 3% against the yuan (all of which occurred recently), and 8% against the peso.

These differing amounts of depreciation are partly a reflection of the countries' willingness to let their currencies fluctuate against the dollar. The euro is free floating, the yen has been moderately managed (mostly before 2005 but more deliberately since September 2010), and the yuan is actively managed (its value rigidly fixed to the dollar before 2005 and from mid-2008 until mid-2010; since then allowed to rise moderately against the dollar).[2] But the pattern also reflects significant structural asymmetries in flows of global assets and global goods, as well as differences in business cycles, inflation rates, shocks affecting the different economies, and an unwinding of imbalances that were present in 2002.[3]

The weakening of the dollar raises concern in Congress and among the public that the dollar's decline is a symptom of broader economic problems, such as a weak economic recovery, rising public debt, and a diminished standing in the global economy. Have recent policy actions such as quantitative easing by the Federal Reserve (Fed) and fiscal stimulus passed by the 111th Congress had an effect on the dollar? How might failure by the 112th Congress to raise the federal debt ceiling or address the country's long-term government debt problem affect the exchange rate? Is there a positive side to dollar depreciation?

Economic theory suggests that the dollar's path can be influenced by a variety of factors that could confer to the United States both benefits and costs, and in some circumstances a depreciating currency can be, on balance, beneficial. This report examines the several factors that are likely to influence the dollar's medium-term path; why further depreciation could occur; what effects a depreciating dollar could have on the economy, including the pace of economic recovery; and how alternative policy measures might influence the dollar's path.

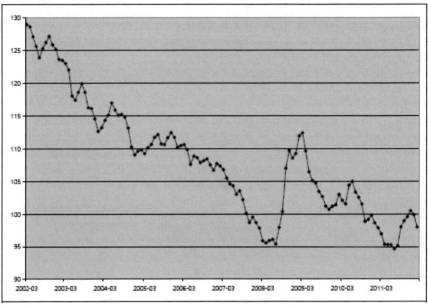

Source: Board of Governors of the Federal Reserve System.

Figure 1. Index of Trade-Weighted Exchange Rate of Dollar.

BROAD ECONOMIC FORCES THAT AFFECT THE DOLLAR

Since the break-up of the Bretton Woods international monetary system in 1973, the exchange rate of the dollar has been largely determined by the market—the supply and demand for dollars in global foreign exchange markets. Dollars are demanded by foreigners to buy dollar denominated goods and assets. (Assets include bank accounts, stocks, bonds, and real property.) Dollars are supplied to the foreign exchange markets by Americans exchanging them for foreign currencies typically needed to buy foreign goods and assets.

Since the mid-1990s, the United States has had a growing trade deficit in goods transactions, generating a net increase in the supply of dollars on the foreign exchange markets, thereby exerting downward pressure on the dollar's exchange rate. At the same time, the United States has had an equal-sized surplus in asset transactions, reflecting a net increase in the demand for dollars

The Depreciating Dollar: Economic Effects and Policy Response   105

on the foreign exchange market, thereby exerting upward pressure on the dollar's exchange rate. [4] In most circumstances, however, there is a strong expectation that asset-market transactions will tend to be dominant and ultimately dictate the exchange rate's direction of movement. This dominance is the result of gross asset-market transactions occurring on a scale and at a speed that greatly exceeds what occurs with goods-market transactions. Electronic exchange makes most asset transfers nearly instantaneous and, in most years, U.S.-international asset transactions were two to three times as large as what would be needed to simply finance that year's trade deficit.

In 2007, near the peak of the last economic expansion, the U.S. capital account recorded $1.5 trillion in purchases of foreign assets by U.S. residents (representing a capital outflow) and $2.1 trillion in purchases of U.S. assets by foreign residents (representing a capital inflow). So while the United States could have financed the $702 billion trade deficit in goods and services in 2007 simply by a $702 billion sale of assets to foreigners, U.S. and foreign investors engaged in a much larger volume of pure asset trading.[5]

DETERMINANTS OF THE SIZE AND DIRECTION OF CROSS-BORDER ASSET FLOWS

Economic theory suggests that several economic factors could influence the direction of cross-border asset flows.

Interest Rate Differentials Between the United States and Other Economies

The demand for assets (e.g., bank accounts, stocks, bonds, and real property) by foreigners will be strongly influenced by the *expected rate of return* on those assets. Therefore, differences in the level of interest rates between economies are, other things equal, likely to stimulate international capital flows from countries with relatively low interest rates to countries with relatively high interest rates, as investors seek the highest rate of return for any given level of risk. When inflation rates among economies are similar, the average level of nominal interest rates can be used as a fairly reliable first approximation of the rate of return on an asset in a particular currency.

Rates of return on dollar assets can be influenced by the general performance of the economy as gauged by its ability to sustain a high rate of economic growth and a low rate of inflation. Another potential influence on expected rate of return is the Fed's conduct of monetary policy as it periodically moves interest rates up or down to stabilize the economy. In addition, whether the United States business cycle is synchronous or asynchronous with that of other economies will influence the relative level of interest rates between it and other economies. In general, these relatively short-term interest rate fluctuations will tend to either attract or deter foreign capital flows, particularly in relatively liquid assets.

The rate of return advantage in the U.S. economy may be greater than the spread between market interest rates would suggest, however. A study by the International Monetary Fund (IMF) that focused on return to debt and equity capital for publicly traded companies in the large industrial economies and the developing economies for the decade 1994-2003 found the rate of return in the United States to have been about 8.6% as compared with a G-7[6] average of about 2.4% and an emerging market average of about *minus* 4.7%.[7]

Currently, the combination of substantial economic slack and highly stimulative monetary policy in the United States and other advanced economies has pushed down short-term and long-term interest rates to historically low levels and left virtually no sizable interest rate advantage of dollar assets over assets in the currencies of other G-7 economies. For example, the yields on 10- year government bonds in Germany, Canada, the United Kingdom, and the United States during 2011 have been within a narrow band of 2.5% to 3.0%. Japan, however, has been an outlier among advanced economies, with the yield on 10-year government bonds hovering slightly above 1% over this period. In contrast, many emerging economies are showing much stronger economic performance and asset yields are likely to be substantially above those in the United States and other advanced economies, which could entice many investors to move capital from the advanced economies to the emerging economies. This would exert downward pressure on the currencies of the advanced economies, including the dollar. [8]

Investors' Expectations About the Future Path of the Dollar

Whether a currency's exchange rate will rise or fall in the future can figure prominently in some investors' calculation of what will actually be earned from an investment denominated in another currency. If, for example, the dollar depreciated on average 4% annually for the next several years, then the 2% to 4% average nominal interest rates currently attached to low-risk medium to long-term U.S. securities would offer the foreign investor an expected return of approximately zero or less. (If the expected currency depreciation were greater, the investor would expect to incur a capital loss.) In general, expected dollar depreciation lowers the expected return and reduces the attractiveness of dollar assets to the foreign investor. On the other hand, if the exchange rate is expected to appreciate, the expected gain would be greater than the nominal interest rate attached to the security, making that asset more attractive. Investor expectations will, therefore, tend to act as an accelerant, adding momentum to the exchange rates movement, whether up or down. At the extremes this could be destabilizing, generating sizable overvaluations or under-valuations of a currency.

The dollar's long and generally orderly depreciation between 2002 and 2008 suggests investor expectations about the currency's path did not act as a destabilizing factor. Nevertheless, the prospect of a secular depreciation likely reduced the attractiveness of dollar denominated assets to foreign investors at that time, and if the current depreciation of the dollar is seen as a resumption of that secular depreciation the attractiveness of dollar assets could also continue to be eroded.

Investors Diversifying Their Portfolio of Assets

For any given interest rate differential and level of the exchange rate, international investors are likely to have a desired balance of assets in their portfolios, allocated not only among types of assets but also by the currency the assets are denominated in. As the stocks they hold of particular assets change over time, investors may see the need to rebalance their portfolios, shifting asset flows away from or toward assets denominated in a particular currency.

Such rebalancing can cause exchange rates for the denominating currency to increase or decrease as well.[9] For example, even if dollar assets offer a relatively high return, at some point foreign investors, considering both risk and reward, could decide that their portfolio's share of dollar-denominated assets is large enough. To mitigate exposure to currency risk in their portfolios, investors could slow or halt their purchase of dollar assets and increase their holdings of non-dollar assets. Such a diversification, other things equal, would tend to depreciate the dollar.

How much pure diversification from dollar assets is likely to happen over the near-term is difficult to determine. Nevertheless, with nearly $11 trillion in U.S. securities estimated to be in foreign investor portfolios, diversification toward other currencies could arguably be a factor of growing importance.[10] However, over the near-term, the general economic fragility of other advanced economies could mean there will be a lack of strong alternatives to dollar assets, tending to limit international investors' willingness to diversify into assets denominated in other currencies. On the other hand, the recent strong growth of many emerging economies could make them an increasingly attractive alternative destination for international capital flows.

Other Factors That Influence the International Demand for Dollar Assets

Beyond the standard determinants of risk and reward that are likely to have a strong near-term influence on the relative attractiveness of dollar-denominated assets, the United States has some added advantages that are thought to generate a sustained underlying demand for dollar assets.

The Size and Liquidity of U.S. Asset Markets

Large asset markets, such as those in the United States, offer a great variety of asset types and a high degree of liquidity. This means that these asset markets are able to handle large inflows and outflows of funds with only a small impact on the price of the asset. Recent IMF estimates of the relative size of the asset markets in the advanced economies show that in 2010 the U.S. bond market had a total value of more than $32 trillion (with government bonds accounting for about $11 trillion of that), whereas the United Kingdom, Germany, and Japan had much smaller bond markets with a total value of about $4.7 trillion, $5.4 trillion, and $12 trillion, respectively. In addition, the U.S. stock market has an estimated capitalized value of about $17 trillion, whereas the United Kingdom, Germany, and Japan's equity markets are much smaller, with estimated capitalized values of about $3.6 trillion, $1.4 trillion, and $4.0 trillion, respectively.[11]

A good example of a large highly liquid asset market is that for U.S. Treasury securities, which has been particularly attractive to foreign investors in recent years. Federal Reserve data show that for the week ending February 1, 2012, the U.S. government securities markets had a daily turnover of about $588 billion. Additional evidence of the high liquidity of U.S. government

The Depreciating Dollar: Economic Effects and Policy Response   109

securities market is its typically small bid-ask spreads. On relatively short-term Treasury securities, the spread is usually a few tenths of a cent per $100 dollar face value of the security.[12]

In recent years, the high liquidity of dollar assets has been an attractive feature for foreign central banks, which have been rapidly increasing their holdings of foreign exchange reserves, a substantial portion of which are thought to be dollar assets. The same is true for petroleum exporting countries, which have in recent years needed to store tens of billions of dollars but also to have ready access to those funds with minimal market disruption.

The degree to which market size influences inflows of foreign capital is hard to determine. However, the persistence of large capital inflows to the United States despite already large foreign holdings of dollar assets offering modest interest differentials and the disproportionate share of essentially no-risk and high-liquidity U.S. Treasury securities in foreign holdings suggest that the magnitude of flows attributable to the liquidity advantage of U.S. asset markets is probably substantial. Failure of the U.S. government, however, to address its long-term government debt problem could raise concerns about default risk and quickly degrade the attractiveness of Treasury securities to foreign investors, and tend to weaken the dollar.

U.S. Asset Markets are Often Seen as "Safe Havens"

Many investors may be willing to give up a significant amount of return if an economy offers them a particularly low-risk repository for their funds. The United States, with a long history of stable government, steady economic growth, and large and efficient financial markets, can be expected to draw foreign capital for this reason. The safe-haven-related demand for dollar assets was particularly evident in 2008 (see *Figure 1*), when uncertainty about global economic and financial conditions caused a substantial "flight to quality" by foreign investors that sharply appreciated the dollar. As global markets stabilized in 2009, the safe haven demand abated somewhat, contributing to the nearly 17% depreciation of the dollar from early 2009 through mid-2011. In the second half of 2011, investor concerns about the sovereign debt crisis in Europe is likely the principal force behind a nearly 5% appreciation of the dollar.

The ongoing size of the safe-haven demand for dollar assets is not easy to determine, but the disproportionate share in foreign holdings of U.S. Treasury securities, which markets still consider to be essentially without default risk, suggests that the magnitude of safe-haven motivated flows is probably substantial, capable of periodically exerting sizable upward pressure on the dollar. Again, perceptions of how "safe" dollar assets are likely to be is influenced by how the 112th Congress addresses the federal government's long term debt problem.[13]

The Dollar is the Principal Global "Reserve Currency"

A reserve currency is a currency held in sizable quantities by foreign governments and central banks as part of their holdings of foreign exchange. Unlike private investors, central banks hold foreign exchange reserves primarily for reasons other than expected rate of return. These so-called official holdings generally serve two objectives. First, the accumulation of a reserve of foreign exchange denominated in readily exchangeable currencies, such as the dollar, provides a safeguard against currency crises arising out of often volatile private capital flows. This is most often a device used by developing economies that periodically need to finance short-run balance of payments deficits and cannot fully depend on international capital markets for such finance. In the wake of the Asian financial crisis of 1997-1998, many emerging economies built up large stocks of foreign exchange reserves, a large share of which were denominated in dollars.

Second, official purchases are used to counter the impact of capital flows that would otherwise lead to unwanted changes in the countries' exchange rates. This is a practice used by China and many east Asian economies that buy and sell dollar assets to influence their exchange rates relative to the dollar in order to maintain the price attractiveness of their exports.

Globally, central bank holdings of reserve currency assets have risen sharply in recent years. The IMF reports that from 2002 through the third quarter of 2011, worldwide official holdings of foreign exchange reserves increased from about $2 trillion to more than $10 trillion. Given the dollar's status as the dominant international reserve currency, a large portion of the accumulation was of dollar-denominated assets. IMF data indicate that of the $5.4 trillion of official holdings of which currency composition is known, nearly $3.4 trillion (or 63%) are in dollar assets. [14] In addition, the U.S. Treasury reports that through January 2011, $3.2 trillion (or 68%) of the $4.7 trillion marketable Treasury securities held by foreigners was being held as foreign official reserves.[15] (The total amount of Treasury securities held by the public, foreign and domestic, through January 2012 was about $10.5 trillion.)[16]

In 2011, China was the world's largest holder of foreign exchange reserves, with holdings valued at more than $3.2 trillion,[17] an increase of nearly $3 trillion since 2002. The exact currency composition of China's foreign exchange reserves is not made public, but the dollar share is thought to

The Depreciating Dollar: Economic Effects and Policy Response   111

be large because that accumulation is largely the consequence of China's buying dollar assets to stabilize the value of its currency relative to the dollar.

Japan is the second largest holder of foreign exchange reserves, with holdings valued at about $1.3 trillion; however, these reserves were largely accumulated prior to 2005.[18] Japan has not in recent years actively tried to influence the value of its currency; nevertheless, dollar assets are thought to be a large share of its reserves. But on March 17, 2011, Japan announced that it would, in concert with other Group of 7 (G-7) nations, intervene in currency markets to stabilize the value of the yen.

The Japanese currency had spiked following the earthquake on March 11, 2011, threatening to stall Japan's exports and deliver another blow to an economy already staggering from that disaster. Japanese officials believed that the yen's sudden strength was being driven by speculation that Japan's firms and financial institutions would soon be bringing back a large portion of their overseas investments to fund Japan's reconstruction. The intervention entailed the selling of yen-denominated assets, tending to push down its value relative to other G-7 currencies, such as the dollar. This was the first joint currency intervention by the G-7 countries in over a decade.[19]

Since the third quarter of 2010, however, the total accumulation of dollar assets by foreign central banks has slowed moderately. Of the $1.2 trillion increase in global foreign exchange reserves for the four quarters ending in the third quarter 2011, dollar holdings increased $220 billion, or represented a share of slightly over 18%, well below the rate in earlier time periods.[20]

How Will These Determinants Interact to Affect the Dollar?

At any point in time, all of the above factors will exert some amount of upward or downward pressure on the value of the dollar, often pushing in opposite directions, making it difficult to disentangle them from their net effect on the dollar. It is difficult to explain with clarity or predict with precision the dollar's near-term path (i.e., several weeks to several months ahead). However, it is possible to assess the general disposition of the forces (as discussed above) likely to influence the dollar in 2012 and 2013.

The following factors point to near-term depreciation of the dollar:

- Low interest rates and slow economic growth in the United States, particularly in comparison to emerging economies, likely lowers the relative expected rate of return on dollar assets.

- International holdings of dollar assets is high and prudent portfolio management could lead to diversification toward other currencies.
- A substantial trade deficit in goods continues to exert downward pressure on the dollar.
- If concerns about euro area sovereign debt problems abate, this will likely reduce recent safe-haven-motivated inflows for dollar assets.
- A growing inflation problem could induce China to slow accumulation of dollar reserves and let its currency rise relative to the dollar.

LIKELY EFFECTS OF DOLLAR DEPRECIATION

Standard economic analysis suggests that a sustained depreciation in the value of the dollar in international exchange has several likely effects, positive and negative, on the U.S. economy.

A Smaller Trade Deficit

The exchange rate determines the relative price of domestic goods and foreign goods, thus it can influence the value and volume of exports sold and imports bought and, in turn, influence the trade balance. Because a depreciating dollar improves the price competitiveness of U.S. exports in foreign markets and deteriorates the price competitiveness of foreign goods in U.S. markets, it will tend to reduce the U.S. trade deficit.[21]

A smaller trade deficit is likely to have two favorable effects on the U.S. economy: first, it will subtract less from demand in the economy, providing a boost to employment; and second, it will slow the growth of U.S. foreign indebtedness. In an economy that still has substantial economic slack, stronger U.S. exports increase domestic economic activity and boost employment; weaker imports represent a rechanneling of domestic spending away from foreign goods and toward domestic goods, which also increases domestic economic activity and boosts employment.

Because the U.S. trade deficit is financed by borrowing from the rest of the world (as evidenced by an equal sized net inflow of foreign capital), a smaller trade deficit will slow the rise of an already substantial net foreign

The Depreciating Dollar: Economic Effects and Policy Response   113

indebtedness and could temper the associated concern about a rising external debt service burden.

The period 1985-1991 was the last time a substantial dollar depreciation and trade deficit adjustment occurred. At that time, the dollar fell a cumulative 40% from a historically high level. In response, the trade deficit started to narrow within two years of the initial depreciation, falling from 3.5% of GDP to near balance by 1991.

For the period 2002-2007, despite a large depreciation of the dollar, the adjustment process has been much slower, with the trade deficit only tipping down modestly in 2007. However, the depreciation of the dollar was having an impact. Economic research suggests that in the United States, depreciation is likely to have a quicker and stronger impact on exports than on imports.[22] This seems to have occurred. Real (non-petroleum) exports began to accelerate in 2003 (the first full year of dollar depreciation) and would continue to grow at a nearly 10% annual rate through 2006 (the year the trade deficit peaked).[23]

The slow effect of the depreciating dollar on the trade balance was the result of import volumes continuing to grow. Again, economic research suggests that U.S. imports have a relatively muted response to exchange rate changes, with a dollar depreciation more likely to slow their growth rather than cause them to decrease. However, in this period several other factors worked to increase imports above what otherwise might be expected and caused a particularly slow response of the trade deficit to the depreciation of the dollar. First, the rapid shift in trade in recent years toward low-cost emerging economies has tended to erode U.S. price competiveness and offset, in part, the competiveness improving effect of the depreciating dollar. Second, up to 2006 the U.S. economy was growing faster than most other advanced economies, tending to boost U.S. imports. Third, oil prices rose to historic highs, increasing the trade deficits of oil-importing countries, such as the United States. (Because the international price of oil is denominated in dollars, dollar depreciation does not directly affect oil's price in the U.S. market. However, some argue it directly contributes to commodity price inflation. This possible relationship is discussed in the "World Commodity Prices (in Dollars) Tend to Increase" section below.)

The U.S. trade deficit in 2010 increased to $470 billion and based on three-quarters of available data should be near that level in 2011 as well.[24] The deficit's increase from 2009's recession induced low of $378 billion was to be expected in a recovering economy, as rising economic activity at home and abroad increased goods and asset flows to more normal levels. In particular, the rebuilding of inventories by U.S. businesses, typical in the early stages of economic recovery, drew in a sizable volume of imports. But that process is transitory and likely already substantially completed. With the dollar already at a relatively competitive level and with strong growth occurring in most emerging economies, there may be strong demand for U.S. exports. Barring a major spike in oil prices or an unlikely surge in spending by U.S. consumers, the trade deficit could stabilize for the near-term at about $500 billion. Any further dollar depreciation will give added momentum to exports and will raise the prospect that the trade deficit could fall over the next few years and help to boost the rate of economic growth.

U.S. International Purchasing Power Decreases

The rising price of imports relative to exports caused by a depreciation of the dollar reduces the purchasing power of U.S. consumers and businesses that purchase imports. To judge the combined effect of export and import price changes on U.S. international purchasing power, economists use the change in the *ratio of export prices to import prices* or what is called *the terms of trade*. For the 26% dollar depreciation that began in early 2002 and ended in mid-2008, the U.S. terms of trade for the same period decreased by approximately 13%.[25]

A 13% decrease in the terms of trade is substantially less than the depreciation of the dollar, which reflects changes in factors in addition to the exchange rate. One factor of particular significance is the effect of changes in producer profit margins. To preserve market share in the U.S. market, importers have shown a tendency to not completely pass through exchange rate depreciations to the dollar price of their products, absorbing a portion of the exchange rate change through slimmer profit margins. This practice substantially mutes the currency depreciation's negative effect on U.S. purchasing power. Also likely muting the impact of a fall in the terms of trade on total purchasing power is the relatively small importance of imports in U.S. gross domestic product (GDP), which only total about 16%.

The dollar value of the loss of purchasing power caused by the dollar's depreciation from 2002 to 2008 can be estimated by comparing the growth of real GDP to the growth of real *command-basis* gross national product (GNP). Command-basis GNP measures the goods and services produced by the U.S. economy in terms of their international purchasing power. In particular, it adjusts the value of real exports to reflect changes in their international purchasing power due to changes in the U.S. terms of trade. Thus, when the

The Depreciating Dollar: Economic Effects and Policy Response   115

terms of trade ratio decreases because of dollar depreciation, real command-basis GNP falls relative to the normally calculated real GDP.[26] From early 2002 through mid-2008, real GDP increased a cumulative $1.9 trillion as compared with command-basis real GDP increasing about $1.6 trillion. The difference of about $300 billion is the estimated loss of international purchasing power due to the dollar's 26% depreciation for that time period.

U.S. Net External Debt Is Reduced

A depreciating dollar tends to improve the U.S. net foreign debt position. This improvement is caused by favorable valuation effects on U.S. foreign assets. These occur because U.S. foreign liabilities are largely denominated in dollars, but U.S. foreign assets are largely denominated in foreign currencies. Therefore, a real depreciation of the dollar increases the value of U.S. external assets and largely does not increase the value of U.S. external liabilities. This asymmetry in the currency composition of U.S. external assets and liabilities means that a dollar depreciation tends to reduce U.S. net external debt.[27]

Exchange rate induced valuation effects are substantial because they apply to the entire stock of U.S. foreign assets, valued at about $20.3 trillion in 2010. The large scale of U.S. foreign assets means that valuation changes can offset a sizable portion of the current account deficit's annual addition to the existing stock of external debt. For example, in 2006, the current account deficit reached a record $811.4 billion. As this was financed by foreign borrowing, it made a like-sized contribution to U.S. external debt. However, the total value of net external debt in 2006 increased only about $300 billion because valuation changes caused the value of the stock of U.S. foreign assets to increase by more than $500 billion. Nearly half of this offset was attributable to positive valuation effects on U.S. foreign assets that were attributable to the dollar's depreciation during that year. In 2007, the impact of valuation changes, including $444 billion caused by dollar depreciation, was sufficiently large to cause the U.S. net external debt to fall despite having to finance a $638 billion current account deficit that year.[28]

World Commodity Prices (in Dollars) Tend to Increase
The fall of the dollar from 2002 to 2007 coincided with large increases in commodity prices. The price of gold increased from about $300 per ounce to more than $600 per ounce, the price of oil increased from about $20 per barrel to near $140 dollars per barrel, and the index of nonfuel commodity prices

rose about 85%.[29] Because most commodities in international markets are priced in dollars, their prices to the U.S. buyer are not directly affected by movements of the exchange rate.

However, a 2008 IMF analysis argues that the dollar does have an indirect impact on commodity prices, that works through at least three channels. First, a dollar depreciation makes commodities, usually priced in dollars, less expensive[30] in non-dollar countries, encouraging their demand for commodities to increase. Second, a falling dollar reduces the foreign currency yield on dollar denominated financial assets, making commodities a more attractive investment alternative to foreign investors. Third, a weakening dollar could induce a stimulative monetary policy in other countries, particularly those that peg their currencies to the dollar. A stimulative monetary policy tends to decrease interest rates, which could stimulate foreign demand, including that for commodities.

The IMF study estimated that if the dollar had remained at its peak of early 2002, by the end of 2007, the price of gold would have been $250 per ounce lower, the price of a barrel of crude oil would have been $25 a barrel lower, and nonfuel commodity prices would have been 12% lower.[31]

Other factors were likely more direct and important causes of the rapid climb of commodity prices at this time. Large increases in world industrial production, particularly in emerging Asian economies, have likely been a factor pulling up commodity prices. Also low interest rates in the United States have reduced the incentive for current extraction over future extraction and generally lowered the cost of holding inventories, dampening the supply response to higher commodity prices.

OTHER POSSIBLE EFFECTS OF DOLLAR DEPRECIATION

Other impacts of a depreciating dollar are more problematic, but are potential risks.

U.S. Interest Rates Could Increase

A falling dollar itself does not directly affect interest rates in the United States. However, the underlying international capital flows that influence the dollar may also influence conditions in domestic credit markets. A weakening of the demand for dollar-denominated assets by private investors tends to

The Depreciating Dollar: Economic Effects and Policy Response 117

depreciate the dollar. A weaker demand for dollar assets is also a likely consequence of a decrease in the net inflow of foreign capital to the U.S. economy. Other things equal, a smaller net inflow of foreign capital reduces the supply of loanable funds available to the economy, tending to increase the price of those funds, that is, increase interest rates.

At this time, however, other things are not equal. The economy, while recovering from the 2008- 2009 recession, still retains substantial economic slack and the demand for loanable funds by businesses and households remains particularly weak. In addition, at least through late 2014, the Federal Reserve appears committed to a policy of monetary stimulus that will keep interest rates low.[32]

However, as economic slack decreases as the recovery progresses, the Fed will likely steadily reduce the amount of monetary stimulus and the domestic demand for credit will likely increase to a more normal level, and together this will exert more upward pressure on interest rates. That pressure will be greater to the degree that domestic savings does not increase sufficiently to offset the reduced inflow of foreign capital (i.e., a reduced supply of loanable funds), making it likely that, coincident with the falling dollar, U.S. interest rates would tend to rise more than they otherwise would.

This added upward pressure on U.S. interest rates could be prevented if there was also an increase in the supply of domestic saving generated by households and the government, sufficient to offset the diminished inflow of foreign capital. Also, rising U.S. interest rates could feedback to improve the relative attractiveness of dollar assets to some foreign investors, tending to slow the net outflow of capital, decrease upward pressure on interest rates, and dampen the rate of dollar depreciation. If, as noted above, the capital outflow is being motivated by other factors in addition to the level of U.S. interest rates, then this feedback effect is not likely to stop the outflow, only slow it.

Dollar's Reserve Currency Role Could Be Reduced

Foreign central bank holdings of reserve currency assets have risen sharply over the past decade. These "official holdings" have nearly quadrupled since 1997, increasing from about $2 trillion to more than $10 trillion by the end of 2011. Of the $5 trillion of official holdings of which currency composition is known, nearly $3 trillion (or 60%) is in dollar assets.[33] Euro-denominated assets have the second largest share at about 25%.

For the United States, there are significant benefits from the dollar being the world's primary reserve currency. Central banks' demand for the reserve currency tends to be less volatile than that of private investors. This stabilizes the demand for dollars and reduces the foreign exchange risk faced by U.S. companies in their international transactions. Exchange rate risk is also reduced because the United States borrows in its own currency, so that the appreciation of foreign currencies against the dollar cannot increase debt-service cost or raise default risk. Another major benefit of having the primary international reserve currency is that it enables the United States to borrow abroad at a lower cost than it otherwise could. This cost advantage occurs because there is a willingness of foreign central banks to pay a liquidity premium to hold dollar assets. Also, the dollar's status as the world's reserve currency raises the incidence of foreigners using U.S. asset markets. This added foreign involvement increases the breadth and depth of these markets, which tends to attract even more investors, which further magnifies the benefits of issuing the reserve currency.

However, the prospect of substantial further depreciation of the dollar could erode the dollar's ability to provide the important reserve currency function of being a reliable store of value. Foreign central banks may see the erosion of this function as a growing disincentive for using the dollar as their principal reserve currency. Another potential threat is any perceived unsustainability of the U.S. long-term debt problem that may eventually result in a downgrading of the U.S. sovereign-risk rating.

Yet, so far there appears to be only modest diversification from dollar assets by foreign central banks. The dollar share of official reserves reached a peak value of about 72% in 2001. Over the subsequent decade this share has slowly decreased, stabilizing at about 62% in 2009 and 2010. The principal alternative to the dollar as a reserve currency has been the euro. Since its creation in 1999, the euro share of global official reserves rose from about 18% to 27% in 2007; however, since then the euro has not increased its share of global reserve assets.[34]

Despite the problems posed for some by the dollar's ongoing depreciation, at present there is arguably no alternative currency to assume its role as principal reserve currency. The sovereign debt crisis in Europe is likely to have diminished the euro's attractiveness to central banks. In addition, the size, quality, and stability of dollar asset markets, particularly the short-term government securities market in which central banks tend to be most active, continues to make dollar assets attractive. A further advantage is the power of "incumbency" conferred by the important "network-externalities" that accrue

The Depreciating Dollar: Economic Effects and Policy Response   119

to the currency that is currently dominant. Together these factors will likely inhibit for the medium-term a large or abrupt change in the dollar's reserve currency status. Nevertheless, over the long-term, many economists predict that a multiple currency arrangement is likely to emerge involving, in addition to the dollar, a continued role for the euro and a substantially increased role of China's yuan. This presumes that China will be able to greatly improve the size and liquidity of its financial markets and create attractive financial instruments. Sustained dollar depreciation could accelerate this process by encouraging more active movement away from dollar assets by central banks.[35]

Risk of a Dollar Crisis Could Be Increased

Although asset market trade offers opportunities to raise overall economic efficiency and improve the economic welfare of borrower and lender alike, trade in assets is prone to occasional volatility, the disorderly resolution of which can lead to financial disruption and, more broadly, a slowing of economic growth. The essential weakness of asset markets is that assets are a claim on a stream of earnings over time—and the future is always uncertain. This can mean that relatively small changes in investors' beliefs about that future could have large effects on the value of the asset. Historically, this has tended to make these markets much more volatile than goods markets, in which value is generally far less contingent on the uncertainties of the future. Add to this the often observed tendency for "herd-like" behavior among investors, particularly those focused on the short run, and the volatility in asset markets can grow larger. Then add in leveraged purchases, the inherent weakness of modern fractional-reserve banking, exchange rate risk, and the usual problems of distance (i.e., different language, law, and business practices) and the potential for volatility and crisis becomes even larger.

There is no precise demarcation of when a falling dollar might move from being an orderly decline to being a crisis, but the depreciation would be significantly more rapid than the orderly fall that has already occurred. The troubling characteristic of a dollar crisis would be that this adjustment could move from orderly to disorderly, due to a precipitous decline in the willingness of investors to hold dollar assets, causing a sharp decrease in the price of those assets and an equally sharp increase in the interest rates attached to those assets. A sudden spike in interest rates could slow domestic interest rate sensitive spending more quickly than the falling dollar can stimulate net exports. This negative impulse could cause overall economic activity to slow, perhaps to the point of stalling the economic recovery.

One factor governing whether dollar depreciation is an orderly or disorderly adjustment is investor expectations about future dollar depreciation. Rational expectations will have a stabilizing effect on the size of international capital flows. The rational forward-looking investor will have some notion of the equilibrium exchange rate and whether the currency is currently overvalued or undervalued. Such investors would only hold assets that have expected yields high enough to compensate for the expected depreciation and also preserve a competitive rate of return.

In contrast, a sharp plunge of the dollar could occur if most investors do not form rational expectations about a likely future depreciation of the dollar. Once investors come to realize that the dollar is falling at a faster rate than they had expected, there could be a sudden attempt by large numbers of investors to sell their dollar assets. But with many sellers and few buyers, the exchange rate would fall precipitously, along with the price of dollar assets, before stabilizing.

Some economists argue that foreign investors do not appear to have built a rational expectation of future dollar depreciation into the nominal yields they are accepting to hold dollar assets. The average nominal rate of return on low-risk treasury securities is currently about 2.5% and in 2010 the dollar depreciated at about a 4% annual rate, so that the ex-post rate of return for foreigners holding these securities has been negative.[36]

If many holders of dollar assets conclude their expectations for dollar depreciation had been too low and try to move quickly out of dollar assets, the ensuing stampede could potentially cause a dollar crisis. A buyer is needed to shed dollar assets, but in a crisis environment this may require a precipitous bidding down of the price of the less desirable dollar assets. This leads not only to a sharply falling exchange rate, but also to sharply rising interest rates in U.S. financial markets (lower asset prices translate into higher effective interest rates).

The dollar, of course, has been on a depreciating trend since 2002, and foreign investors have continued to hold dollar assets for which the attached interest rate seems insufficient to compensate for that depreciation. But there has been no dollar crisis. The avoidance of crisis is, perhaps, explained in part by the large accumulation of dollar reserves by foreign central banks. If foreign central banks have longer investment horizons than private investors, they will tend to stabilize the demand for dollar assets. In general, the large size and stability of the dollar-asset markets (along with the ongoing needs of central banks and other international investors) for liquidity and a store of value undergirds the strong persistent international demand for dollar assets.[37]

POLICIES THAT COULD INFLUENCE THE DOLLAR

Does the United States Have a Dollar Policy?

Treasury Secretaries have in the past asserted that the United States has a "strong dollar policy," but have rarely taken direct steps to influence the dollar's value.[38] As noted earlier, since the 1973 demise of the Bretton Woods fixed exchange rate international monetary system, the de facto U.S. dollar policy has been to let market forces determine the dollar's value. The collapse of that monetary system was to a large degree due to its increasing inability to maintain fixed-exchange rates in the face of the massive growth of international capital flows in a reintegrated and rapidly growing post-war global economy.[39]

Mainstream economic theory suggests that a country cannot be open to large international capital flows (as the United States is) and directly control both its exchange rate and its interest rates. Because the management of interest rates is seen as central to the overriding policy goal of stabilizing the domestic economy to maintain high employment and low inflation, the U.S. Federal Reserve and the central banks of most other advanced economies control interest rates and, therefore, have implicitly decided to let their exchange rates fluctuate, more or less, freely.

The exchange rate, while usually not the primary target, can be affected by macroeconomic policies, such as quantitative easing, fiscal stimulus, and debt reduction. Its movement might well support achieving these broader macroeconomic goals, but a particular level for the exchange rate has not been an explicit policy goal in the United States. However, occasionally the government has acted to directly influence the exchange rate. In addition, government policies, programs, and institutions that undergird a "strong U.S. economy" arguably exert a indirect positive effect on the dollar.

Policies to Influence the Demand for U.S. Assets

Given the importance of international asset markets in determining the dollar's exchange rate, policies aimed at directly or indirectly influencing the demand and supply of dollar assets would potentially have the greatest direct impact on the dollar.

Direct Intervention in the Foreign Exchange Market

This policy involves the Federal Reserve at the request of the Treasury buying or selling foreign exchange in an attempt to influence the dollar's exchange rate. (This intervention will most often be *a sterilized* intervention that alters the currency composition of the Fed's balance sheet but does not change the size of the monetary base, neutralizing any associated impact on the money supply.) To strengthen the dollar, the Fed could attempt to boost the demand for dollars by selling some portion of its foreign exchange reserves in exchange for dollars. (Sterilization in this case would require the Fed to also purchase a like value of domestic securities to offset the negative effect on the monetary base of its selling of foreign exchange reserves.)

The problem with intervention is that the scale of the Fed's foreign exchange holdings is small relative to the size of global foreign exchange markets, which have a *daily* turnover of more than $4.0 trillion.[40] Facing markets of this scale, currency intervention by the Fed would likely be insufficient to counter a strong market trend away from dollar assets and prevent depreciation of the dollar.

A coordinated intervention by the Fed and other central banks would have a greater chance of success because it can increase the scale of the intervention and have a stronger influence on market expectations. Since 1985, there have been six coordinated interventions: the Plaza Accord of 1985 to weaken the dollar, the Louvre Accord of 1987 to stop the dollar's fall, joint actions with Japan in 1995 and 1998 to stabilize the yen/dollar exchange rate, G-7 action in 2000 to support the newly introduced euro, and G-7 action in 2011 to limit appreciation of the Japanese yen. All but the Louvre Accord do correspond with turning points for the targeted currencies.

However, these interventions were most often accompanied by a change in monetary policy that was consistent with moving the currencies in the desired direction. Many economists argue that coordinated intervention in these circumstances played the useful role of a signaling device helping overcome private investors' uncertainty about the future direction of monetary policy and the direction the central banks want the currency to move. But absent an accompanying change in monetary policy it is unlikely that even coordinated intervention would be successful at altering the exchange rate's trend if it were being strongly propelled by private capital flows.

Monetary Policy

The Federal Reserve uses monetary policy to influence economic conditions. By increasing or decreasing interest rates, it tightens or loosens credit conditions.[41]

Changing the level of interest rates can also influence the dollar's exchange rate. A tighter monetary policy would tend to strengthen the dollar because higher interest rates, by making dollar assets more attractive to foreign investors, other things equal, boosts the demand for the dollar in the foreign exchange market. In contrast, lower interest rates would tend to weaken the dollar by reducing the attractiveness of dollar assets. In either case, however, it would be unprecedented for the Fed to use monetary policy to exclusively target the exchange rate, but it could be the side-effect of policies aimed at controlling inflation or stimulating aggregate spending to speed economic recovery.

In general, a floating exchange rate gives the central bank greater autonomy to use monetary policy to achieve domestic stabilization goals. In the current macroeconomic situation, if the Fed were obligated to prevent the dollar from depreciating, it would likely be constrained from applying the degree of monetary stimulus needed to promote economic recovery.

It is likely that the Fed's current policy of monetary stimulus to sustain economic recovery, by keeping interest rates low, has exerted downward pressure on the dollar as well. Although not the primary target of this monetary policy, the incidental depreciation of the dollar contributes to the Fed's stabilization goal of boosting economic growth by providing a boost to net exports.

Fiscal Policy and Federal Debt

Government choices about spending and taxing can also influence the exchange rate. Budget deficits tend to have a stimulative effect on the economy. However, because the government must borrow funds to finance a budget deficit, it increases the demand for credit market funds, which, other things equal, tends to increase interest rates. Higher interest rates will tend to increase the foreign demand for dollar-denominated assets, putting upward pressure on the exchange rate.

However, in the current state of the U.S. economy, with a sizable amount of economic slack and weaker than normal private demand for credit market funds, current government borrowing does not appear to have elevated market interest rates, and, therefore, does not appear likely to exert upward pressure on the exchange rate. Moreover, the likely prospect of a slower than normal economic recovery suggests a substantial amount of economic slack and relatively weak private demand for credit is likely to persist over the near term. These conditions will continue to mute the interest elevating effect of currently anticipated government borrowing and continue to exert minimal upward pressure on the dollar.

As economic recovery moves the U.S. economy closer to full employment and the private demand for credit market funds increases, continuing large government budget deficits may result in higher interest rates. Some foreign investors could be attracted by these higher interest rates, increasing their demand for dollar assets. This would exert upward pressure on the dollar.

However, if the federal government does not implement a credible solution to its long-term debt problem, it is possible that the expectation of persistent large budget deficits and sharply rising public debt could degrade the expected long-term performance of the U.S. economy by crowding out productive investment and slowing the pace of economic growth. This anticipated deterioration could reduce international investors' expected rate of return on dollar assets, accordingly reduce the long-term demand for dollar assets. This reduced demand would exert downward pressure on the dollar's international exchange value.

Putting in place a credible program of fiscal consolidation would also have an ambiguous effect on the dollar's longer-term path. Less government borrowing would tend to lower interest rates and depreciate the dollar, while the improved prospect for long-term growth and expected rates of return would tend to appreciate the dollar.

Policies to Increase the Demand for U.S. Exports

Policies that tend to increase the foreign demand for U.S. goods and services also tend to strengthen the dollar.

Lower Foreign Trade Barriers
The continued existence of various trade barriers in many countries may keep the demand for U.S. exports weaker than it otherwise would be. If lowering those barriers significantly boosts the demand for U.S. goods and services, it would also exert some upward pressure on the dollar exchange rate. It is difficult to judge how strong this upward pressure would be. Moreover, this is not likely to be a readily implementable policy tool and probably has little near-term significance for the dollar's exchange rate.

The Depreciating Dollar: Economic Effects and Policy Response   125

Support for Development of New Products

If the United States has goods and services that are strongly in demand in the rest of the world, there will be some upward pressure on the exchange rate. Economic theory suggests that the government's role in this process is to support those aspects of research and development that are likely to be under-invested in by the private market. This type of policy would most likely have long-run implications, but not have much effect on the near-term value of the dollar.

Indirect Government Influence on the Dollar

Over the long run, at least three factors will likely continue to indirectly support the international demand for dollar assets: (1) the basic economic performance of the U.S. economy as measured by GDP growth, productivity advance, and pace of innovation has for the past 25 years been superior to that of Japan and the major euro area economies;[42] (2) the Fed is widely seen as a credible manager of monetary policy and has a strong record of maintaining macroeconomic stability; and (3) the large and highly liquid U.S. asset markets will likely continue to be an attractive destination for foreign investors. Therefore, decisions by the 112th Congress regarding policies that enhance or degrade any of these three attributes of the U.S. economy will accordingly tend to indirectly strengthen or weaken the dollar's long-term path. Of likely immediate relevance is the near term issue of sustaining economic recovery and reducing unemployment and the long-term issue of reducing the growth of federal debt.

GLOBAL IMBALANCES, THE DOLLAR, AND ECONOMIC POLICY

As already discussed, the dollar's exchange rate largely reflects fundamental economic forces, particularly those that influence the demand for and supply of assets on international financial markets. Currently, an examination of those forces highlights a large and potentially destabilizing imbalance in the global economy: in the United States persistent large trade deficits and the accumulation of foreign debt, and in the rest of the world large trade surpluses, weak domestic demand, and the accumulation of dollar denominated assets. Most economists would argue that this is a condition that carries more than a negligible risk of generating financial instability and eventual global economic crisis.

To achieve an orderly correction of these imbalances that assures more stable exchange rates and leaves all the involved economies on sounder macroeconomic footing, mainstream economic thinking suggests that the needed rebalancing can be most efficiently achieved by a coordinated international policy response, the salient elements of which are

- in the United States, raising the national saving rate via substantial increases in the saving rates of households and government and through that reducing the U.S. trade deficit to a "sustainable" size;[43]
- in Japan and Europe, generating faster economic growth primarily propelled by domestic spending rather than net exports;
- in Asia (excluding Japan and China), fostering a recovery of domestic investment and reducing the outflow of domestic saving; and
- in China (and other surplus economies that fix their exchange rates to the dollar), allowing their currencies to appreciate and channel more of their domestic savings into domestic spending.[44]

A key attribute of such a rebalancing of global spending would likely be further depreciation of the dollar. This outcome illustrates that an orderly depreciation of the dollar can be, on balance, a beneficial attribute of policy adjustments and economic changes that would ultimately improve economic conditions in the United States and abroad. There is some evidence that a global rebalancing is in progress. In the United States, the saving rate of households is up and the federal government seems to be moving toward raising public saving by reducing its long-term deficit problem. In China, the yuan has appreciated and the government's recently released five-year plan points to that country undertaking policies to raise its domestic consumption and narrow its global trade surplus.[45]

End Notes

[1] The trade-weighted exchange rate index used is the price-adjusted broad dollar index reported monthly by the Board of Governors of the Federal Reserve System. The real or inflation-adjusted exchange rate is the relevant measure for gauging effects on exports and imports. A trade-weighted exchange rate index is a composite of a selected group of currencies, each dollar's value weighed by the share of the associated country's exports or imports in U.S.

trade. The broad index cited here is constructed and maintained by the Federal Reserve. The broad index includes the currencies of 26 countries comprising 90% of U.S. trade and, therefore, the broad index is a good measure of changes in the competitiveness of U.S. goods on world markets.

[2] See CRS Report RL33577, U.S. International Trade: Trends and Forecasts, by Brock R. Williams and J. Michael Donnelly, for more data and charts on exchange rates.

[3] Data on bilateral exchange rates are available at Board of Governors of the Federal Reserve System, Federal Reserve Statistical Release H.10, http://www.federalreserve.gov/ releases/ h10/hist/.

[4] The current account is a tally of international purchases (imports) and sales (exports), and the current account balance measures the country's net exports of goods and services. The capital account is a tally of international purchases and sales of dollar denominated assets, and the capital account balance measures the country's net foreign investment. If the capital account is in surplus, foreigners are investing more in the United States then Americans are investing abroad, leading to a net inflow of capital. Because every purchase of a foreign good or asset requires the payment of a domestic good or asset, net flows in the current account and the capital account will be equal and offsetting. Therefore a current account deficit must be matched by an equal capital account surplus, and a current account surplus by a capital account deficit. The exchange rate adjusts to make this so.

[5] See U.S. Department of Commerce, Bureau of Economic Analysis, U.S. International Economic Accounts, 2007, Table 1, http://www.bea.gov/international/bp_web/list.cfm? anon=71&registered=0.

[6] The G-7 refers to the periodic Group of Seven finance ministers and central bank governors conference. The seven countries represented are Canada, Japan, France, Germany, Italy, the United Kingdom, and the United States.

[7] International Monetary Fund, World Economic Outlook, Global Imbalances: In a Saving and Investment Perspective, September 2005, pp. 100-104.

[8] Organisation for Economic Co-operation and Development (OECD), Economic Outlook 90, Annex Table 35, Long-Term Interest Rates, http://www.oecd.org/document/61/0,3746,en_ 2649_34573_2483901_1_1_1_1,00.html.

[9] Prudent investment practice counsels that the investor's portfolio of asset holdings have not only an appropriate degree of diversification across asset types, but also diversification across the currencies in which the assets are denominated. Moving from a relatively undiversified investment portfolio to a more diversified one spreads risk, including exchange rate risk, across a wider spectrum of assets and helps avoid over- exposure to any one asset.

[10] U.S. Department of the Treasury, Report on Foreign Portfolio Holdings of U.S. Securities, Table 1, April 13, 2011, http://www.treasury.gov/resource-center/data-chart-center/tic/ Documents/shla2010r.pdf.

[11] IMF, Global Financial Stability Report, October 2011, Statistical Appendix, Table 3, http://www.imf.org/External/ Pubs/FT/GFSR/2010/02/pdf/statappx.pdf.

[12] Federal Reserve Bank of New York, Primary Dealer Transactions in U.S. Government Securities, February 23, 2011, http://www.newyorkfed.org/markets/statistics/deal.pdf.

[13] On the demand for safe assets see Ben S. Bernanke, 'International capital flows and the returns to safe assets in the United States 2003-2007, Financial Stability Review, Banque de France, no. 15, February 2011, http://www.banquefrance.fr/gb/publications/telechar/rsf/ 2011/etude02_rsf_1102.pdf.

[14] In contrast, the United States in this time period held foreign exchange reserves of less than $200 billion on average, with annual increments of only $1 billion to $10 billion. See IMF, Currency Composition of Official Foreign Exchange Reserves, December, 2011, http://www.imf.org/external/np/sta/cofer/eng/cofer.pdf.

[15] U.S. Department of the Treasury, Treasury International Capital System (TIC), Major Foreign Holders of Treasury Securities, http://www.treasury.gov/resource-center/data-chart-center/tic/Documents/mfh.txt.

[16] U.S. Department of the Treasury, Treasury Direct, Dept to the Penny, http://www.treasury.gov/resource-center/data chart-center/tic/Documents/mfh.txt.

[17] Statistics on Chinese international reserves are from Chinability, a nonprofit provider of Chinese economic and business data, http://www.chinability.com/Reserves.htm.

[18] Japan, Ministry of Finance, December 28, 2011, http://www.mof.go.jp/english/e1c006.htm.

[19] Binyamin Appelbaum, "Goup of 7 to Intervene to Stabilize the Yen's Value," New York Times March 17, 2011, http://www.nytimes.com/2011/03/18/business/global/18group.html.

[20] IMF, Currency Composition of Official Reserves, December 30, 2011, http://www.imf.org/external/np/sta/cofer/eng/ cofer.pdf.

[21] This effect is likely to be evident first on real trade flows (the volume of exports and imports) and more slowly on nominal trade flows (the current dollar value of exports and imports). This differential effect on real and nominal flows occurs because the higher relative price of imports has two impacts. On the one hand, domestic consumers buy a reduced volume of foreign goods, while on the other hand, each unit of the foreign goods is valued higher in terms of dollars. Initially, the volume effect can be dominated by the value effect, causing the nominal trade balance to not fall or perhaps even rising for a period in response to a depreciating exchange rate. Ultimately, the volume effect could come to dominate the value effect and the nominal trade deficit would also begin to fall.

[22] International Monetary Fund, World Economic Outlook September 2007, Chapter 3, "Exchange Rates and the Adjustment of External Imbalances."

[23] U.S. Census Bureau, U.S. International Trade Data, http://www.census.gov/foreign-trade/statistics/historical/ realpetr.pdf.

[24] Bureau of Economic Analysis, U.S. International Transactions Account, Table 1, line 77, http://www.bea.gov/ international/bp_web/simple.cfm?anon=71&table_id=1&area_id=3.

[25] Bureau of Economic Analysis, National Economic Accounts, Table 1.8.6, http://www.bea.gov/national/nipaweb/ SelectTable.asp?Selected=N.

[26] Ibid.

[27] Most countries are not able to borrow in their own currency, so a fall of their exchange rate will tend to increase their net external debt. This was a problem that plagued the economies caught in the Asian financial crisis in 1997, when their crashing currencies ballooned the home currency value of their external debt.

[28] Data for U.S. net external debt are compiled annually and the most recent estimate is for 2010. For further details on net external debt and valuation effects see U.S. Department of Commerce, Bureau of Economic Analysis, U.S. Net International Investment Position for Yearend 2010, June 2011, http://www.bea.gov/international/index.htm#bop.

[29] IMF Primary Commodity Prices, February 2011, http://www.imf.org/external/np/res/commod/Table1-020911.pdf.

[30] Assuming their currency is not pegged to the dollar.

[31] International Monetary Fund, World Economic Outlook – April 2008, pp. 48-50.

[32] Board of Governors of the Federal Reserve System, Federal Reserve Press Release, January 25, 2012, http://www.federalreserve.gov/newsevents/press/monetary/20120125a.htm.

The Depreciating Dollar: Economic Effects and Policy Response 129

[33] IMF, Currency Composition of Official Foreign Exchange Reserves, December, 2011, http://www.imf.org/external/ np/sta/cofer/eng/cofer.pdf.

[34] Ibid, IMF.

[35] For further discussion of this issue, CRS Report RL34083, The Dollar's Future as the World's Reserve Currency: The Challenge of the Euro, by Craig K. Elwell.

[36] U.S. Department of the Treasury, 2010 Average Historical Monthly Interest Rates, http://www.treasurydirect.gov/ govt/rates/pd/avg/2010/2010.htm.

[37] For more discussion of this issue, see CRS Report RL34311, Dollar Crisis: Prospect and Implications, by Craig K. Elwell.

[38] See for example Keith Bradsher, New York Times, August 17, 1995, "Treasury Chief Says Strong Dollar Isn't a Threat to Trade," http://www.nytimes.com/1995/08/17/ business/ international-business-treasury-chief-says-strongdollar-isn-t-a-threat-to-trade.html; USA Today, August 1, 2006, " New Treasury secretary backs strong dollar, Social Security solution", http://www.usatoday.com/money/economy/2006-08-01-paulson-speech_x.htm; and Tom Patrino, Los Angles Times, November 12, 2009, " Treasury Secretary Tim Geither pays lip service to keeping dollar strong," http://articles.latimes.com/keyword/lip-service.

[39] On post-war global capital flows and the demise of the Bretton Woods system, see Barry Eichengreen, Globalizing Capital: A History of the International Monetary System(Princeton University Press, 1996), pp. 93-135.

[40] Bank of International Settlements, Triennial Central Bank Survey of Foreign Exchange and OTC Derivatives Market, September 11, 2010, http://www.bis.org/press/p100901.htm.

[41] Since 2008, the policy interest rate has been at its minimum, called the "zero bound." The Federal Reserve has taken other nonconventional measures to further stimulate the economy. These are described in CRS Report RL30354, Monetary Policy and the Federal Reserve: Current Policy and Conditions, by Marc Labonte.

[42] The World Economic Forum in its 2010 Global Competitiveness Report ranks the United States as the fourth most competitive economy in the world and the United States has been at or near the top of this ranking since it began in 1979, http://www3.weforum.org/ docs/WEF_GlobalCompetitivenessReport_2010-11.pdf.

[43] A trade deficit is arguably sustainable if it does not cause the U.S. foreign debt/GDP ratio to rise. For the United States a trade deficit as a percent of GDP of 2% or less would probably meet this sustainability criterion. For further discussion of sustainability see CRS Report RL33186, Is the U.S. Current Account Deficit Sustainable?, by Marc Labonte.

[44] On global rebalancing, see for example: Olivier Blanchard, "Sustaining Global Recovery," International Monetary Fund, September 2009, http://www.imf.org/external/pubs/ft/fandd/ 2009/09/index.htm; "Rebalancing," The Economist, March 31, 2010, http://www.economist.com/node/15793036; and Board of Governors of the Federal Reserve System, Vice-chairman Donald L. Kohn, Speech "Global Imbalances," May 11, 2010, http://www.federalreserve.gov/ newsevents/speech/kohn20100511a.htm.

[45] China Daily, October 28, 2010, "China's Twelfth Five-Year Plan signifies a new phase in growth," http://www.chinadaily.com.cn/bizchina/2010-10/27/content_11463985.htm and Martin Feldstein, "The End of China's Surplus, Project Syndicate, January 28, 2011, http://www.project-syndicate.org/commentary/feldstein32/English.

In: Exchange Rates and Currency Debates ISBN: 978-1-62948-616-1
Editor: Darren Byers © 2013 Nova Science Publishers, Inc.

Chapter 4

CURRENCY MANIPULATION: THE IMF AND WTO*

Jonathan E. Sanford

SUMMARY

Congress has been concerned, for many years, with the possible impact that currency manipulation has on international trade. The International Monetary Fund (IMF) has jurisdiction for exchange rate questions. The World Trade Organization (WTO) is responsible for the rules governing international trade. The two organizations approach the issue of "currency manipulation" differently. The IMF Articles of Agreement prohibit countries from manipulating their currency for the purpose of gaining unfair trade advantage, but the IMF cannot force a country to change its exchange rate policies. The WTO has rules against subsidies, but these are very narrow and specific and do not seem to encompass currency manipulation. Recently, some have argued that an earlier ruling by a WTO dispute resolution panel might be a way that currency issues could be included in the WTO prohibition against export subsidies. Congress is currently considering legislation to amend U.S. countervailing duty law, based on this precedent, that the proponents believe is consistent with WTO rules. Others disagree as to whether the previous case is a sufficient precedent.

---

* This is an edited, reformatted and augmented version of a Congressional Research Service publication, CRS Report for Congress RS22658, prepared for Members and Committees of Congress, from www.crs.gov, dated January 28, 2011.

Several options might be considered for addressing this matter in the future, if policymakers deem this a wise course of action. The Articles of Agreement of the IMF or the WTO Agreements could be amended in order to make their treatment of currency manipulation more consistent. Negotiations might be pursued, on a multilateral as well as a bilateral basis, to resolve currency manipulation disputes on a country-by-country basis without changing the IMF or WTO treatment of this concern. Some countries might argue that the actions of another violate WTO rules and seek a favorable decision by a WTO dispute resolution panel. Finally, the IMF and WTO could use their interagency agreement to promote better coordination in their treatment of this concern.

INTRODUCTION

This report describes how the International Monetary Fund (IMF) and World Trade Organization (WTO) deal with the issue of currency manipulation. It also discusses apparent discrepancies in their charters and ways those differences might be addressed.

INTERNATIONAL MONETARY FUND

The IMF is the leading international organization in the area of monetary policy. With the end of the cold war, its membership is now nearly universal. Only North Korea, the Vatican, and four other mini-countries in Europe— none having its own currency—are not members of the Fund. The IMF makes loans to countries undergoing financial or balance of payments crises; provides technical assistance to governments on monetary, banking and exchange rate questions; does research and analysis on monetary and economic issues; and it provides a forum where countries can discuss international finance issues and seek common ground on which they can address common problems.

Although the IMF is a monetary institution, the promotion of world growth and balanced international trade are also among its basic goals. Article I of its Articles of Agreement says, among other things, that the IMF was created in order to "facilitate the expansion and balanced growth of international trade, and to contribute thereby to the promotion and maintenance of high levels of employment and real income and to the development of the productive resources of all members as primary objectives of economic policy." It was also created to "assist in the establishment of a

Currency Manipulation: The IMF and WTO   133

multilateral system of payments in respect to current transactions between members and in the elimination of foreign exchange restrictions which hamper the growth of world trade."

Between 1946 and 1971, the IMF supervised a fixed parity exchange rate system, in which the value of all currencies was defined in terms of the U.S. dollar and the dollar was defined in terms of a set quantity of gold. Countries could not change their exchange rates from the level recognized by the IMF by more than 10% without the Fund's consent. Moreover, said the original language of the IMF Articles, "A member shall not propose a change in the par value of its currency except to correct fundamental disequilibrium."[1] This system broke down in 1971 when the United States devalued the dollar twice without any consultation with the IMF. After a period of turmoil in world currency markets, an amendment to the IMF Articles was adopted in 1978. It said that countries could use whatever exchange rate system they wished—fixed or floating—so long as they followed certain guidelines and they did not use gold as the basis for their currencies.

The new language of Article IV, which went into effect in 1978, said that countries should seek, in their foreign exchange and monetary policies, to promote orderly economic growth and financial stability and they should avoid manipulation of exchange rates or the international monetary system *to prevent effective balance of payments adjustment or to gain unfair competitive advantage over other members.*[2] Some countries claim that their exchange rate policies are not in violation of Article IV because they are not seeking to gain competitive advantage (though this may be the result of their actions) but rather *to stabilize the value of their currency in order to prevent disruption to their domestic economic system.* To date, the IMF has not publicly challenged this statement of their objective.

The Fund was required by Article IV to "exercise firm surveillance over the exchange rate policies of all members and [to] adopt specific principles for the guidance of all members with respect to those policies." The IMF adopted the requisite standards in 1977 (before the Amendment went into effect) and it updated them in 2007. The 1977 agreement said that, among other things, "protracted large-scale intervention in one direction in exchange markets" might be evidence that a country was inappropriately manipulating the value of its currency. The 2007 agreement added a requirement that "A member should avoid exchange rate policies that result in external instability." When a country's current account (balance of payments) is not in equilibrium, the IMF said in its explanation of the new provision, the exchange rate is "fundamentally misaligned" and should be corrected.[3]

The IMF can exercise "firm surveillance" but it cannot compel a country to change its exchange rate. Nor can it order commercial foreign exchange dealers to change the prices at which they trade currencies. It can offer economic advice and discuss how changes in countries' exchange rates might be in their own interest. It can also provide a forum, such as its new multilateral consultation mechanism or discussion on the IMF executive board, where other countries can urge a country to change its exchange rate procedures. However, in the end, the authority to make the change resides with the country alone.

WORLD TRADE ORGANIZATION

The WTO is the central organization in the world trade system. When the WTO was created in 1995, countries were required to accept as a condition of WTO membership the existing trade rules embodied in the General Agreement on Tariffs and Trade (GATT). They also had to accept new rules governing other areas of international commerce, such as services and trade-related international property rights. The agreement establishing the WTO says that the members recognize "that their relations in the field of trade and economic endeavor should be conducted with a view to raising standards of living, ensuring full employment and a steady growing volume of real income and effective demand, and expanding the production of and trade in goods and services" and to do this in a manner "consistent with their respective needs and concerns at different levels of economic development."[4]

Unique among the major international trade and finance organizations, the WTO has a mechanism for enforcing its rules. If a country believes another country has violated WTO rules, to its detriment, it may request the appointment of a dispute settlement panel to hear its complaint. The other country cannot veto the establishment of a panel or adoption of a WTO decision by WTO members. The panel reviews the arguments in the case and renders judgment based on the facts and WTO rules. If the losing party does not comply with the ruling within a reasonable period of time, the WTO may, if requested by the complaining party, authorize it to impose retaliatory measures (usually increased customs duties) against the offending country or to take other appropriate retaliatory measures against that country's trade.

Whether currency disputes fall under the WTO's jurisdiction is a debatable issue. The WTO rules specify that countries may not provide subsidies to help promote their national exports. Most analysts agree that an undervalued currency lowers a firm's cost of production relative to world prices and therefore helps to encourage exports. It is less clear, however, whether intentional undervaluation of a country's currency is an export subsidy under the WTO's current definition of the term.[5] Countries are entitled, under WTO rules, to levy countervailing duties on imported products that receive subsidies from their national government.

The term "subsidy" has a precise definition in the WTO. It requires that there must be a financial contribution by a government to the exporter or some other form of income or price support. Government financial support can take a variety of forms, such as direct payments to the exporter, the waiver of tax payments or special government purchases or the provision of low-cost goods or services (other than general infrastructure) that lowers the cost of production. Currency manipulation would not appear to qualify under the WTO definitions. In addition, an export subsidy is a subsidy that is "contingent on export performance." They must also be "specific to an industry" and not provided generally to all producers.[6] In the past, most legal analysts have found that intentional undervaluation of a currency is not a subsidy that is "contingent on export performance" and not "industry specific" because everyone who exchanges currency gets the same rate even if they are not exporting. More recently, other analysts have asserted, based on an interpretation of the findings in a WTO dispute settlement case,[7] that a subsidy may still be export contingent, even if it is available in some circumstances that do not involve exportation. Thus, they believe, subsidies provided through currency misalignment would be a prohibited subsidy under WTO rules even if non-exporters benefit from the exchange rate. Until the world financial system frayed in the 1970s, the IMF exercised strict control over exchange rates. It was inconceivable that a country could persistently value its currency at a level below that approved by the IMF. When the IMF's rules were changed in 1978, so that it no longer governed world exchange rates, the GATT rules were not adjusted to reflect the new reality of international finance. When the WTO was created in 1995, it adopted the existing GATT rules as its own without significant change and without acknowledging that the international system of exchange rates had changed substantially since the GATT was formed.

WTO AND IMF COOPERATION

The WTO and IMF both have major institutional responsibilities in the area of international trade. The WTO, and its predecessor organization, the

GATT, were created specifically to facilitate the negotiation of multilateral trade agreements. One of the corresponding purposes of the IMF is to "facilitate the expansion and balanced growth of international trade" in order to facilitate high levels of employment, economic growth, and development in all its member countries."[8] The WTO seeks to expand international trade through the reduction or elimination of tariffs or other barriers to trade. The IMF pursues this goal mainly through efforts to promote international monetary and exchange rate stability. It also has standards, which it has been reluctant to employ, for determining whether currencies are being manipulated and whether they are valued properly relative to other currencies. Trade policy issues may feature prominently in the IMF's surveillance activities, relative to its member countries, and steps to reduce barriers to trade are often included in its policy advice and its loan conditionality. IMF surveillance reports often provide important contributions for the WTO's own Trade Policy Reviews, which assess its member countries' trade policies.

The IMF and GATT signed an agreement aimed at facilitating inter-agency cooperation soon after the trade organization was formed in 1947. The IMF and WTO adopted a revised and updated version of that agreement in 1996, shortly after the WTO came into being. The two organizations agreed (in paragraphs 1 and 2 of the agreement) that they "shall consult with each other in the discharge of their respective mandates," with a view towards "achieving greater coherence in global economic policymaking."[9] Article XV of the GATT agreement says that the GATT (now WTO) shall cooperate with the IMF in order to "pursue a coordinated policy with regards to exchange questions that are within the jurisdiction of the Fund."

The WTO and IMF also agreed in 1996 (in paragraph 8) that they would communicate with each other about "matters of mutual interest." WTO dispute settlement panels are specifically excluded from this agreement to communicate, but the agreement says that the IMF shall inform the WTO (specifically including its dispute settlement panels) when the WTO is "considering exchange measures within the Fund's jurisdiction [in order to determine] whether such measures are consistent with the Articles of Agreement of the Fund." Earlier (in paragraphs 3 and 4), the IMF agreed that it would inform the WTO about any decisions it had made approving any restrictions a country might impose on international payments, discriminatory currency practices, or other measures aimed at preventing a large or sustained outflow of capital. The IMF also agreed, in 1996, that it would participate in any WTO discussion of any such measures countries may have taken to safeguard their balance of payments.

POLICY OPTIONS IN THE MULTILATERAL SPHERE

A number of countries have been suspected or accused in recent years of manipulating the value of their currency for the purpose of gaining unfair trade advantage.

The George W. Bush and Barak Obama Administrations have had many conversations with China about exchange rate issues. Nonetheless, their officials were careful never to say publicly that China was manipulating its currency in violation of IMF rules. During his confirmation hearing on January 23, 2009, then Treasury Secretary-designate Timothy Geithner reported that "President Obama, backed by the conclusions of a broad range of economists, believes that China is manipulating its currency."

The Obama Administration has not pursued this line of thought, however, in its subsequent public statements on the issue.

If the Treasury Department were to find, in its semi-annual reports to Congress on the topic, that China or any other country were manipulating its currency in order to gain unfair trade advantage, certain provisions of the 1988 trade act would be triggered.

TheSecretary would have to "to initiate negotiations with such foreign countries on an expedited basis, in the International Monetary Fund or bilaterally, for the purpose ofensuring that such countries regularly and promptly adjust the rate of exchange between their currencies and the United States dollar to permit effective balance of payments adjustments and to eliminate the unfair advantage."[10]

The country in question is not required, however, to meet with U.S. officials or to take any corresponding action. U.S. efforts to press China or other countries to revalue their currencies would likely be routed through the IMF, in order to secure its good offices and to mobilize international support on this issue. The 1988 trade act does not require the Administration to take this complaint about currency manipulation to the WTO in order to seek remedies through its procedures.

As noted before, the IMF Articles of Agreement prohibit this currency manipulation for the purpose of gaining unfair trade advantage, but the Fund has no capacity to enforce that prohibition. By contrast, the WTO has the capacity to adjudicate trade disputes, but to date it has done nothing to suggest that trade issues linked to currency manipulation are within its zone of responsibility. If policymakers want to address this situation, several options might be considered.

Amend the Articles of the IMF

One option might be changes in the IMF's Articles of Agreement that would give the Fund more authority over international exchange rates and more authority to require that countries comply with its rules. This would restore, to some degree, the power the IMF exercised over exchange rates from 1946 to 1971. Two objections might be raised, however.

First, an 85% majority vote of the IMF member countries is necessary if any change in the IMF Articles is to become effective. Most countries seem to believe that the present system of floating and fixed exchange rates is working reasonably well and there seems to be little desire, on the part of the members, to amend the IMF's current rules. Second, few countries want the IMF to have the kinds of power over their economies that it would need to compel violators comply with its rules. For example, if the IMF had the power to declare that China's currency was undervalued and to require adjustments, it would also have the power to declare the U.S. dollar or the euro were overvalued and to require the United States or the eurozone countries to make changes in their domestic policies that would bring down the relative value of their currencies.

Amend the WTO Agreements

Another possibility might be a formal change in the WTO agreements that would define currency manipulation as a prohibited form of export subsidy. It is not easy to amend WTO agreements, however, since the process basically requires the unanimous consent of all Members. Countries that manipulate their currencies could easily block the approval of the amendment. However, they might argue that currency manipulation is an acceptable trade practice notwithstanding the language of the IMF's Article IV. It seems more likely that any such change in the WTO rules will be the result of discussions during multilateral trade negotiations, in which restrictions on currency manipulation will be balanced by other changes desired by the countries that believe currency manipulation is an acceptable trade practice.

Pursue Multilateral Negotiations

Recently, the Administration has indicated that it will be raising the issue of misaligned currencies and their impact on international trade at international meetings involving world leaders. Treasury Secretary Timothy Geithner has told Congress on several occasions that the Administration is working through multilateral channels, such as the G-20 meeting of world leaders, the Asia-Pacific Cooperation (APEC) forum, and the IMF to obtain international support for the effort to press China to revalue its currency.[11] It is also seeking discussion about the international financial imbalances and steps that might be taken to address that concern.

The Administration has been talking regularly with the Chinese about this and other related topics for several years. Arguably, resolving the U.S.- China disagreement about exchange rates is a desirable objective. However, one might argue, a bilateral settlement of this dispute would be of only limited value. Unless the agreement among world leaders also includes measures that would make WTO and IMF treatment of these issues more consistent, the question whether undervalued currencies provide improper export subsidies is likely to arise again in the future. A bilateral agreement with China would not preclude other countries from undervaluing their currencies in order to undercut China and get better access to its former export markets.

Obtain Adjudication

One way for the issue to be resolved could be through WTO adjudication of disputes involving the United States and other countries. In the past, currency issues have not been pursued via the WTO dispute settlement process. The United States might seek WTO adjudication of this issue by taking China or other countries to a dispute resolution panel, on the basis of a claim that China's currency policy improperly subsidizes Chinese exports.

Alternatively, the United States could take action under its domestic trade laws to address the problem and let other countries decide what they will do about the issue. Congress is considering legislation (H.R. 2378, reported by the House Ways and Means Committee on September 24, 2010) which would seek to address the question of undervalued exchange rates in a way that the sponsors believe is consistent with WTO rules. It provides that countervailing duties may be imposed to address possible subsidies that might result when other countries' currencies are fundamentally undervalued. It says that these subsidies may be treated as being "contingent upon export performance" (a key element of the WTO definition) even if others not exporting also benefit from the subsidy. If this legislation is enacted into law and duties are levied on Chinese imports, some analysts believe that China will assert that it is inconsistent with WTO rules and will seek remedies through the WTO dispute settlement process.

There may be a role for the IMF in this adjudication process, if world leaders decide that it should be involved. Article II of the GATT agreement says that the valuations used in countries' tariff schedules shall be "expressed in the appropriate currency at the par value accepted or provisionally recognized" by the IMF. Though the par value exchange system is gone, this language might be construed as giving the IMF some role in determining whether the exchange rates used in trade agreements and schedules are appropriate. Currency values may be adjusted, it says, as long as this "will not impair the value of the concessions provided" in trade agreements. This language, as well as similar language in Article VII, dates from before the adoption of the present floating exchange rate system. However, the effect of inappropriate exchange rates on trade agreements seems to be a continuing concern.

Article XV says that, when disputes between signatory countries involve questions about balances of payments, foreign exchange reserves or exchange arrangements, GATT countries shall "consult fully with the International Monetary Fund" and shall accept the IMF's determination as to matters of fact and as to whether a country's exchange arrangements are consistent its obligations under the IMF Articles of Agreement. GATT Article XV also says that countries "shall not, by exchange action, frustrate the provisions of this agreement nor, by trade action, the intent of the provisions" of the IMF Articles of Agreement.

Traditionally, these references to "exchange arrangements" have been seen as referring (as they did when the GATT was created in 1947) to currency controls, exchange licenses, transaction taxes and other official actions that limit a potential purchaser's ability to get the foreign exchange needed to purchase goods from abroad.[12] The GATT allows countries to impose temporary import restrictions when they face balance of payments difficulties (Article XII) or when they are at risk for a serious decline in their foreign exchange reserves (Article XVIII).

In recent decades, however, the term "exchange arrangements" has expanded to reflect new developments in the world economy. The language of Article IV, adopted by the IMF in 1978, says (section 2) that each member country shall notify the IMF of the exchange arrangements it intends to apply – in other words, whether its currency will float in value or be pegged to another currency. It says the IMF shall oversee the international monetary system to ensure that each country's exchange arrangements are compatible with its obligations under Article IV. IMF Article IV also says that, in its oversight of countries' exchange arrangements, the Fund shall exercise firm surveillance over the exchange rate policies of its member countries. In effect, a case can be made that the term "exchange arrangements" arguably has become synonymous with the concept "exchange rate regime" and "exchange rate policies."

As it is used in GATT Article XV, the term "exchange arrangement" refers to issues that are the sole province of the IMF. Thus, one could argue that the meaning of the term in the GATT should reflect its current meaning at the IMF and not the meaning prevalent in 1947. An undervalued currency encourages exports by reducing their cost and it discourages imports by making them more expensive than they might be otherwise. Consequently, one might argue that countries with this type of exchange arrangement are engaging in "exchange action" that may have the effect of frustrating "the provisions of the [GATT] agreement."

There has never been a definitive ruling by the GATT or WTO on the meaning of Article XV, including how provisions of the GATT agreement might be frustrated by exchange action. Some might argue that currency undervaluation raises the price of imports in a way that unilaterally rescinds tariff concessions approved during multilateral trade talks.

Accordingly, a case could be made that the WTO should use the broader meaning of the term "exchange arrangements" and take currency valuation arrangements into account in its dispute settlement process. There has also been increased interest, in recent years, in the issue of currency manipulation and its impact on world trade and financial relationships. It could be argued, therefore, that this might be an appropriate and perhaps auspicious moment for issues relating to the trade impact of currency manipulation to be raised in the WTO dispute adjudication process.

Improve the IMF-WTO Agreement

The final option for rectifying the disconnect between WTO and IMF treatment of currency manipulation issues might involve some change or reinterpretation of the WTO-IMF inter-agency agreement. As noted above, the agreement states they will "cooperate in the discharge of their respective mandates" in order to achieve "greater coherence in global economic policymaking." Arguably, the different ways in which they approach the issue of currency manipulation and its impact on international trade does not further or facilitate such "greater coherence." The member countries of the two institutions might encourage them to identify other occasions where their rules and procedures are not consistent or mutually supportive.

Changes in the existing inter-agency agreement can be adopted by a majority vote of each institution's governing board. However, it is not clear that changes in the text of the agreement are needed to promote greater cooperation between the two institutions. Paragraph 14 of the agreement says that the "Director-General of the WTO and the managing Director of the Fund shall be responsible for the implementation of this Agreement and, to that effect, shall make such arrangements as they deem appropriate."

The GATT Agreement and the WTO-IMF inter-agency agreement both give the IMF a role in WTO dispute settlement procedures. A more up-to-date interpretation of those agreements, which take into account changes that have taken place during the intervening years in IMF operations and procedures, might help address some of the concerns discussed above.

The IMF no longer determines par values for national currencies. Nevertheless, it does have standards and procedures for determining whether currencies are appropriately valued or whether they are being manipulated inappropriately. Consequently, the language in Articles II and IV of the GATT Agreement, in which currency values and exchange rate procedures must be consistent with the Articles of the IMF, would seem to give the IMF some role in any WTO discussions about whether currency manipulation "impairs the value of the concessions provided" in trade agreements. Likewise, as Article XV of the GATT Agreement seems to give the IMF plenary authority to determine whether the "exchange arrangements" used by the parties to the dispute are consistent with IMF requirements. The way the GATT now interprets the term "exchange arrangements" appears to be antiquated and it seems to predate the meaning which the IMF now gives to that term. Agreement by the leaders of the two institutions that they will use a consistent meaning of the term might help diminish some of the apparent inconsistencies in their operations.

Even if the meaning of the inter-agency agreement is adjusted, as discussed above, to reflect the contemporary functions of the IMF, however, the IMF can play a role advising the WTO about exchange and currency manipulation issues only if it takes an official position on the question in hand. To date, the IMF has consulted with China behind the scenes and it has used its good offices to facilitate multilateral discussions, involving China, the United States, and several other relevant countries, as regards the appropriate

Currency Manipulation: The IMF and WTO

valuation of China's currency. No official action has been taken by the IMF on this issue.

As noted previously, the IMF has no way of enforcing decisions it might make as to whether countries are complying with the exchange rate provisions of Article IV. The IMF has adopted standards which make the requirements of Article IV operational, but it has not used those standards officially to assess the activities of particular countries. Perhaps the IMF's member countries are concerned that its prestige might be injured if the IMF Executive Board made an official determination that a country was manipulating its currency, in violation of its obligations in the IMF, and nothing happened as a result. A decision of this sort could be more meaningful, however, if it were to be the basis of information the IMF could provide to the WTO about the currency exchange aspects of disagreements that were being examined by a dispute settlement panel. Adjusting the terms of the inter-agency agreement between the IMF and WTO, or reinterpreting the meaning of that agreement in the light of current practices, might be one option policy makers could use to address the trade implications of currency manipulation.

End Notes

[1] International Monetary Fund, Articles of Agreement. This language is quoted from Section 5 of the original language of Article IV as approved by the 1944 Bretton Woods conference and confirmed by all member countries when the IMF officially came into existence in 1946. The Terms of Article IV were subsequently changed by the Second Amendment, which was adopted in 1976 and entered into force in 1978.

[2] Ibid., Section 3 (iii) in the language of Article IV which became effective in 1978. It allows countries to maintain fixed rates or to adopt floating or market-based rates of exchange for their national currencies. The IMF must approve the exchange system countries adopt but it no longer has a role in determining relative currency values.

[3] IMF. IMF Surveillance—the 2007 Decision on Bilateral Surveillance. Factsheet, June 2007.

[4] Agreement Establishing the World Trade Organization, 1995, preamble.

[5] Agreement on Subsidies and Countervailing Measures, Articles 1 to 3.

[6] WTO Agreement on Subsidies and Countervailing Measures, Articles 2-3.

[7] See WTO, Dispute Settlement 108: United States – Tax Treatment for "Foreign Sales Corporations," at http://www.wto.org/english/tratop_e/dispu_e/cases_e/ds108_e.htm. The legislation reported by the House Ways and Means Committee on September 24, 2010 (see below) is based on this interpretation of WTO rules.

[8] IMF Articles of Agreement, Article I, subsection ii.

[9] Agreement Between the International Monetary Fund and the World Trade Organization, Paragraph 2, republished in IMF, Selected Decisions and Selected Documents of the International Monetary Fund, 31st Issue, Washington, D.C. December 31, 2006. The preamble to the agreement acknowledges that there are increasing links between the issues

addressed by the two institutions and it notes that the Marrakesh Agreement, establishing the WTO, called for greater coherence internationally in economic policies.

[10] Exchange Rates and International Economic Policy Coordination Act of 1988, Sec. 5304 of the Omnibus Foreign Trade and Competitiveness Act of 1988, P.S. 100-418, August 23, 1988.

[11] U.S. Treasury. Testimony of Treasury Secretary Timothy Geithner. China's Currency Policies and the U.S.-China Economic Relationship. Testimony before the Senate Banking Committee and House Ways and Means Committee. September 16, 2010, at http://www.treasury.gov/press-center/press-releases/Pages/tg858.aspx.

[12] See, for example, John H. Jackson, World Trade and the Law of GATT. New York: The Bobbs-Merrill Company, 1969, pp. 479-495.

INDEX

A

access, 23, 45, 55, 78, 100, 109, 139
accounting, 47, 72, 74, 95, 99, 108
adjustment, 13, 23, 26, 37, 64, 67, 74, 77, 80, 82, 83, 94, 96, 113, 119, 120, 133
aggregate demand, 18, 75, 76, 77
Algeria, 95
alters, 122
anger, 56
Angola, 95
annual rate, 50, 55, 90, 113, 120
antidumping, 38, 60, 61, 62, 97
Argentina, 36, 37, 95
Asia, 3, 4, 79, 86, 97, 126, 139
Asian countries, 86
assessment, 13, 66, 67
assets, x, 6, 7, 12, 18, 38, 45, 62, 75, 76, 82, 83, 89, 100, 102, 103, 104, 105, 106, 107, 108, 109, 110, 111, 112, 115, 116, 117, 118, 119, 120, 122, 123, 124, 125, 127
asymmetry, 115
Austria, 34
authorities, 35, 56, 61
authority, 4, 27, 134, 138, 142
autonomy, 123
avoidance, 30, 120
Azerbaijan, 95

B

Bahrain, 27
balance of payments, 23, 26, 37, 55, 75, 96, 110, 132, 133, 136, 137, 140
balance sheet, 122
Bank of England, 18, 34, 38
banking, 83, 93, 119, 132
banks, 7, 80, 93, 99, 110, 118, 120
barriers, 44, 84, 124, 136
base, ix, 19, 41, 76, 122
Belgium, 34
benchmarks, 38, 54
beneficiaries, 76
benefits, ix, 8, 29, 42, 44, 77, 79, 80, 103, 118
bilateral, 5, 37, 62, 143
black market, 45
Bolivia, 95
bond market, 108
bonds, x, 12, 13, 17, 18, 19, 29, 99, 102, 104, 105, 106, 108
BOP, 60
borrowers, 75, 82, 86
Brazil, viii, 2, 3, 10, 16, 17, 18, 28, 29, 33, 34, 36, 37, 88
Bretton Woods conference, 143
Bretton Woods system, 129
budget deficit, ix, x, 29, 42, 76, 82, 88, 98, 102, 123, 124

146 Index

Bureau of Labor Statistics, 98
Bush, George W., 137
business cycle, 99, 103, 106
businesses, vii, viii, 1, 11, 29, 53, 113, 114, 117
buyers, 116, 120

C

capital account, 35, 37, 45, 94, 105, 127
capital controls, 12, 18, 24, 72, 82, 83, 100
capital flight, 94
capital flows, 6, 7, 8, 16, 29, 62, 75, 76, 105, 108, 110, 116, 120, 121, 122, 127, 129
capital inflow, 60, 64, 76, 77, 105, 109
capital markets, 6, 110
capital outflow, 82, 83, 91, 94, 105, 117
Caribbean, 34
Census, 128
central bank, xi, 6, 7, 13, 15, 17, 19, 21, 27, 45, 46, 64, 65, 75, 76, 82, 83, 102, 109, 110, 111, 117, 118, 120, 121, 122, 123, 127
challenges, 65, 85
Chile, 27
Chinese firms, 44, 73, 75, 79, 91, 99
Chinese government, 12, 43, 44, 45, 46, 48, 50, 56, 73, 78, 80, 82, 85, 91, 93, 96, 99
circulation, 17
citizens, 75, 82, 83, 94, 100
clarity, 111
classification, 29
coastal region, 81
coherence, 136, 141, 144
cold war, 132
Colombia, 27
combined effect, 114
commerce, 134
commercial, 19, 85, 134
commercial bank, 19
commodity, x, 7, 101, 113, 115, 116
compensation, 100
competition, 80

competitive advantage, viii, 23, 26, 27, 38, 41, 53, 54, 55, 64, 96, 133
competitiveness, viii, 2, 3, 4, 13, 26, 27, 28, 32, 112, 127
compliance, 27
composition, 16, 76, 94, 110, 115, 117, 122
conference, 43, 63, 127
Congress, v, viii, x, xi, 1, 2, 3, 4, 19, 22, 25, 26, 27, 28, 30, 31, 32, 33, 35, 36, 37, 38, 41, 42, 43, 55, 56, 57, 58, 59, 61, 63, 84, 100, 101, 102, 103, 110, 125, 131, 137, 139
Congressional Budget Office, 88
consensus, 30, 32, 67
consent, 36, 133, 138
Consolidated Appropriations Act, 38
consolidation, 124
constant rate, 12
consumer price index, 49, 92, 95
consumers, vii, viii, ix, 1, 5, 6, 10, 11, 17, 29, 32, 34, 42, 44, 70, 71, 75, 81, 99, 114, 128
consumption, 21, 51, 73, 75, 77, 84, 86, 90, 91, 93, 99, 100, 126
conversations, 137
cooperation, 25, 30, 33, 64, 85, 136, 142
coordination, xi, 22, 25, 132
correlation, 54
cost, 5, 10, 11, 24, 29, 44, 51, 54, 71, 83, 91, 99, 113, 116, 118, 135, 141
countervailing duty, xi, 57, 58, 61, 96, 131
credit market, 123, 124
crises, ix, 16, 42, 110, 132
critical period, 93
criticism, 53
crowding out, 124
crude oil, 116
current account, ix, 35, 37, 42, 45, 50, 51, 53, 55, 56, 62, 63, 66, 67, 69, 70, 75, 76, 84, 85, 86, 88, 89, 95, 98, 100, 115, 127, 133
current account balance, 50, 67, 86, 88, 95, 98, 100, 127
current account deficit, 53, 62, 67, 69, 70, 75, 76, 86, 87, 88, 89, 100, 115, 127

Index

147

current account surplus, ix, 42, 50, 51, 55, 56, 67, 70, 84, 87, 88, 89, 95, 100, 127

Cyprus, 34

D

danger, 54
data availability, 66
database, 92
debt service, 113
decision-making process, 22
deficit, 54, 70, 71, 83, 88, 89, 96, 105, 112, 113, 115, 126, 127, 129
deflation, 19, 20
Denmark, 15, 53
Department of Commerce, 62, 96
Department of the Treasury, 55, 65, 96, 97
deposits, 73, 82, 91, 92
depreciation, x, 19, 20, 25, 47, 48, 54, 67, 101, 103, 107, 109, 111, 112, 113, 114, 115, 116, 117, 118, 119, 120, 122, 123, 126
depth, 118
devaluation, 11, 27, 34, 55, 99
developed countries, viii, 2, 3, 11, 18, 19, 21, 89
developing countries, 45
developing economies, 106, 110
direct payment, 135
disaster, 111
disequilibrium, 34, 36, 133
displacement, 54
disposable income, 92
disposition, 111
distortions, 16
distribution, 74
diversification, xi, 102, 107, 108, 112, 118, 127
domestic credit, 116
domestic demand, 17, 64, 73, 117, 125
domestic economy, 21, 81, 121
domestic investment, 85, 87, 88, 126
dominance, 105
Dominican Republic, 27
dual exchange rate, 45, 55

dumping, 57, 60, 99

E

earnings, 119
East Asia, 44, 86
economic activity, 112, 113, 120
Economic and Monetary Union, 34
economic change, 67, 126
economic crisis, ix, 41, 51, 95, 126
economic development, 50, 55, 81, 134
economic downturn, 89
economic efficiency, 44, 81, 119
economic fundamentals, 9, 16, 25, 63, 64, 100
economic growth, ix, 11, 23, 42, 44, 51, 53, 74, 75, 77, 78, 81, 84, 85, 86, 91, 93, 99, 106, 109, 111, 114, 119, 123, 124, 126, 133, 136
economic institutions, 84
economic losses, 84
economic performance, x, 16, 101, 106, 125
economic policy, xi, 93, 102, 132, 136, 141
economic problem, x, 101, 103
economic reform, 81, 85, 93
economic reforms, 85, 93
economic theory, 54, 72, 75, 76, 121
economic welfare, 75, 119
economic well-being, 75, 100
economics, 67, 99
economies of scale, 73
Ecuador, 9
education, 93, 100
effective exchange rate, 5, 38, 49, 58, 59, 62, 63, 66, 97
elasticity of demand, 98
emerging markets, viii, 2, 3, 17, 18
emerging-market currencies, viii, 2, 3
employment, 16, 18, 54, 73, 74, 76, 77, 85, 96, 98, 99, 112, 121, 132, 136
employment levels, 74
encouragement, 62
enforcement, 27, 28, 30, 99
environment, 45, 120
environmental standards, 99

148   Index

equilibrium, 9, 16, 27, 29, 59, 61, 63, 66, 67, 68, 79, 97, 98, 120, 133
equipment, 75, 89
equity, 106, 108
equity market, 108
erosion, 118
Estonia, 34
EU, 4, 34, 36, 37, 95
Europe, 14, 35, 36, 84, 93, 103, 109, 118, 126, 132
European Central Bank, 14, 18
European Union, 4, 34, 36, 37, 95
evidence, 13, 16, 50, 67, 76, 108, 126, 133
evolution, xi, 102
excess demand, 45
exchange rate pegs, 7
exchange rate policy, 34, 74, 86
exercise, 133, 134, 141
expenditures, 73, 99
export market, 86, 139
export sector, vii, viii, 1, 10, 44, 80, 97
export subsidies, xi, 24, 58, 131, 139
exporter(s), vii, viii, ix, 1, 10, 31, 41, 42, 45, 60, 70, 73, 76, 83, 95, 96, 97, 100, 135
export-led growth, 10
exposure, 107, 127
expulsion, 23
external liabilities, 115
externalities, 118
extraction, 116

F

factor endowments, 63
factories, 46, 71
FDI, 78, 79
FDI inflow, 79
fear, 7, 82
fears, 28, 82, 94
federal government, x, 60, 82, 102, 110, 124, 126
Federal Register, 97
Federal Reserve, 18, 36, 61, 73, 99, 103, 104, 108, 117, 121, 122, 123, 126, 127, 128, 129

financial, vii, viii, ix, 1, 2, 10, 12, 13, 15, 17, 18, 23, 25, 28, 32, 37, 42, 44, 46, 54, 55, 61, 62, 65, 73, 80, 84, 85, 86, 94, 96, 100, 102, 109, 110, 111, 116, 119, 120, 125, 128, 132, 133, 135, 139, 141
financial condition, 109
financial crisis, vii, ix, 1, 10, 12, 13, 15, 17, 18, 25, 32, 42, 44, 46, 54, 55, 85, 86, 102, 110, 128
financial instability, 126
financial institutions, 111
financial markets, 109, 119, 120, 125
financial sector, 84
financial stability, 23, 65, 133
financial support, 135
financial system, 94, 135
Finland, 34
fiscal policy, 76
fixed exchange rates, 8, 24, 99, 138
fixed rate, 143
flexibility, 12, 44, 46
flight, 109
floating exchange rates, 7, 8, 10, 34, 67, 100
fluctuations, 16, 46, 100, 106
force, xi, 80, 99, 109, 131, 143
foreign capital flows, 106
foreign companies, 73
foreign direct investment, 51
foreign exchange, ix, x, xi, 6, 7, 12, 13, 15, 16, 17, 21, 23, 25, 35, 42, 43, 45, 50, 53, 55, 60, 64, 70, 80, 94, 95, 102, 104, 109, 110, 111, 118, 122, 123, 128, 133, 134, 140
foreign exchange market, x, 6, 7, 12, 13, 15, 16, 17, 25, 102, 104, 122, 123
foreign firms, 71
foreign investment, 79, 127
fragility, 108
France, 25, 34, 36, 37, 88, 127
free markets, vii, viii, 1
free trade, 3, 4, 27, 30
full employment, 77, 88, 124, 134
funding, 23
funds, 80, 108, 109, 117, 123, 124

Index 149

G

GAO, 26, 38, 56
garbage, 19, 53
GATT, 24, 37, 134, 135, 136, 140, 141, 142, 144
GDP, 5, 9, 13, 50, 52, 53, 55, 64, 67, 73, 76, 79, 84, 85, 87, 88, 89, 90, 92, 93, 94, 95, 100, 113, 114, 125, 129
General Agreement on Tariffs and Trade, 24, 134
Germany, 25, 34, 36, 37, 86, 88, 106, 108, 127
global competition, 81
Global Competitiveness Report, 129
global demand, 46, 51, 84, 86
global economy, x, 2, 3, 4, 10, 11, 16, 18, 29, 30, 31, 32, 50, 51, 65, 74, 77, 79, 85, 101, 103, 121, 125
global markets, x, 102, 109
global recession, 88
global trade, 126
GNP, 114
goods and services, 34, 37, 50, 70, 73, 75, 80, 81, 95, 99, 100, 105, 114, 124, 125, 127, 134
government budget, 86, 124
government intervention, 12, 32
government securities, 108, 118
governments, 7, 9, 17, 32, 62, 100, 110, 132
GPA, 60
grants, 4
graph, 14
Great Depression, 11
Greece, 34
gross domestic product, 114
gross investment, 86, 90
gross national product, 114
growth, x, 10, 11, 19, 32, 50, 55, 64, 67, 73, 77, 79, 81, 82, 84, 85, 89, 90, 92, 93, 98, 102, 108, 112, 113, 114, 121, 124, 125, 129, 132, 136
growth rate, 82, 90
guidance, 23, 133
guidelines, 23, 62, 133

H

health, 91, 93
health care, 91, 93
history, 109
Hong Kong, 9, 15, 53, 69, 71
host, 19, 25, 26
House, x, 26, 33, 38, 42, 43, 54, 57, 58, 63, 96, 98, 139, 143, 144
House of Representatives, 98
household income, 73
housing, 76, 82, 86
hybrid, 8

I

identification, 59
identity, 72
imbalances, ix, 42, 44, 51, 64, 72, 83, 85, 86, 100, 103, 126, 139
import prices, 71, 72, 98, 114
import restrictions, 140
imported products, 24, 77, 97, 135
imports, vii, viii, ix, 1, 2, 6, 10, 11, 17, 21, 29, 31, 34, 38, 41, 42, 45, 54, 55, 57, 59, 60, 69, 70, 71, 73, 75, 77, 78, 79, 80, 81, 86, 89, 97, 98, 99, 100, 112, 113, 114, 126, 127, 128, 139, 141
import-sensitive goods, vii, viii, 1
incidence, 118
income, 37, 73, 81, 89, 91, 93, 95, 100, 135
India, 16, 36, 37, 88
Indonesia, 36, 37, 88
industrial policies, 44, 73, 84
industrialized countries, 53
industries, 79, 99
industry, 24, 27, 54, 135
inflation, ix, 5, 13, 16, 17, 21, 35, 42, 43, 47, 49, 80, 81, 83, 91, 97, 98, 99, 102, 103, 105, 106, 112, 113, 121, 123, 126
infrastructure, 93, 135
institutions, 25, 29, 32, 33, 121, 142, 144
intellectual property, 44, 84
intellectual property rights, 44, 84

150 Index

interest rates, ix, x, 16, 17, 18, 25, 29, 42, 44, 63, 75, 76, 80, 82, 86, 91, 101, 105, 106, 107, 111, 116, 117, 119, 120, 121, 123, 124
international financial institutions, 30, 38
international investment, 6
international meetings, 139
International Monetary Fund, viii, xi, 2, 22, 36, 50, 55, 58, 87, 88, 96, 98, 99, 106, 127, 128, 129, 131, 132, 137, 140, 143
international trade, xi, 8, 11, 24, 26, 27, 32, 55, 131, 132, 134, 135, 138, 141
intervention, ix, 16, 30, 35, 42, 43, 46, 50, 53, 54, 55, 56, 58, 59, 60, 61, 62, 85, 96, 111, 122, 133
investment(s), ix, xi, 6, 7, 8, 21, 32, 35, 42, 44, 45, 51, 72, 73, 75, 79, 82, 84, 85, 86, 89, 90, 91, 93, 94, 100, 102, 106, 116, 120, 124, 127
investors, xi, 6, 7, 13, 76, 80, 102, 105, 106, 107, 108, 109, 110, 116, 117, 118, 119, 120, 122, 123, 124, 125
Ireland, 34
Israel, 95
issues, vii, xi, 2, 3, 4, 22, 25, 26, 27, 28, 30, 31, 32, 44, 55, 63, 65, 96, 98, 99, 131, 132, 137, 139, 141, 142, 143
Italy, 34, 36, 37, 127

J

Japan, viii, 2, 3, 4, 15, 17, 19, 20, 21, 25, 33, 36, 37, 38, 53, 54, 68, 69, 71, 84, 86, 88, 95, 106, 108, 111, 122, 125, 126, 127, 128
job creation, vii, viii, 1, 10
jurisdiction, xi, 25, 131, 134, 136

K

Kazakhstan, 95
Korea, 38, 53

L

labeling, 28, 29
labor market(s), 99
laws, 28, 57, 58, 139
lawyers, 24
lead, vii, viii, 1, 10, 56, 74, 77, 82, 83, 85, 94, 99, 100, 110, 112, 119
legislation, x, xi, 3, 22, 26, 27, 30, 31, 32, 38, 42, 43, 58, 63, 68, 96, 131, 139, 143
legislative proposals, 44, 57, 63
lending, 73, 93
light, 143
liquid assets, 106
liquidity, x, 62, 102, 108, 109, 118, 119, 121
loans, 80, 84, 93, 132
local government, 82, 93
long-term debt, x, 102, 118, 124
Louvre Accord, 25, 30, 122
lower prices, 44

M

machinery, 71, 79, 81
macroeconomic policies, 121
macroeconomic policy, 77
magnitude, 109
majority, 33, 96, 138, 142
Malaysia, 15, 53, 69, 95
management, 121
manipulation, viii, xi, 2, 4, 22, 23, 26, 28, 29, 30, 31, 32, 33, 37, 38, 50, 53, 54, 55, 56, 96, 100, 131, 132, 133, 135, 137, 138, 141, 142, 143
manufacturing, ix, 41, 43, 44, 54, 75, 91, 99, 100
market access, 84
market economy, 61, 97
market segment, 73
market share, 114
matter, xi, 17, 132
MB, 66, 98
measurement, 47, 49, 66, 95, 100
measurements, 49, 62

media, 78, 99
medical, 100
membership, 22, 132, 134
merchandise, 31, 70, 79, 95
methodology, 68, 96
Mexico, 16, 36, 37, 88
models, 10, 29, 65, 66
momentum, 107, 114
monetary expansion, 53
monetary policy, vii, x, 18, 19, 22, 27, 38, 53, 59, 80, 102, 106, 116, 122, 123, 125, 132
money supply, 16, 17, 18, 19, 59, 80, 83, 99, 100, 122
Morocco, 27
Moscow, 38
Multilateral, 25, 37, 137, 138
multinational corporations, 71, 79

N

negative effects, 32, 44
negotiating, 3, 4, 19, 30, 31, 60
negotiation, 30, 31, 136
net exports, x, 23, 28, 79, 93, 101, 120, 123, 126, 127
Netherlands, 34
New Zealand, 15, 34
North Korea, 19, 36, 132

O

Obama, 33, 43, 54, 63, 64, 76, 96, 137
Obama Administration, 54, 63, 64, 76, 137
Obama, President, 4, 43, 63, 94, 97, 137
obstacles, 30
OECD, 127
officials, 53, 63, 78, 84, 99, 111, 137
oil, 113, 114, 115
operations, 30, 142
opportunities, 81, 119
output gap, 86
overseas investment, vii, 1, 6, 111
Overseas Private Investment Corporation, 60

oversight, x, 102, 141

P

Pacific, 3, 4, 33, 54, 139
Panama, 9, 27
parity, 133
participants, 35
pegging, 45
permission, 94
permit, 55, 137
Peru, 27
petroleum, 71, 109, 113
Philippines, 69, 95
playing, 63
policy issues, x, 101, 136
policy makers, 143
policy options, 4, 32
policymakers, xi, 3, 12, 18, 25, 28, 32, 53, 69, 81, 132, 137
political leaders, 3
portfolio, 107, 112, 127
portfolio management, 112
Portugal, 34
precedent, xi, 131
president, 4, 19, 27, 43, 60, 63, 94, 97, 137
President Obama, 4, 43, 63, 94, 97, 137
prestige, 143
price changes, 70, 114
price index, 70
price stability, 18
principles, 133
private sector, 89
procurement, 60
producers, viii, 3, 24, 31, 32, 41, 70, 73, 82, 98, 99, 135
professionals, 100
profit, 83, 114
profit margin, 114
project, 36, 60, 129
property rights, 134
protection, 44, 73, 74
protectionism, 78
public debt, x, 101, 103, 124
purchasing power, x, 75, 101, 114

Index

R

rate of return, x, 102, 105, 106, 110, 111, 120, 124
rational expectations, 120
raw materials, 71, 79, 81
real estate, 80
real income, 132, 134
real property, x, 102, 104, 105
real terms, 47
real wage, 77, 100
reality, 135
reasoning, 9
recession, vii, 1, 15, 18, 21, 32, 102, 113, 117
reconstruction, 111
recovery, x, 55, 79, 85, 101, 103, 104, 114, 117, 120, 123, 124, 125, 126
reflate, 11
reform(s), 3, 31, 33, 38, 43, 44, 46, 57, 58, 59, 77, 78, 81, 84, 96, 97
reinsurance, 60
relative prices, 6
relative size, 86, 108
relevance, 125
relief, 75
remittances, 37
repression, 73
requirements, 21, 26, 142, 143
reserve assets, 118
reserve currency, x, 101, 110, 117, 118
reserves, ix, xi, 13, 15, 16, 19, 34, 42, 43, 50, 53, 58, 60, 64, 66, 70, 83, 95, 100, 102, 109, 110, 111, 112, 118, 120, 122, 128, 140
resolution, xi, 119, 131, 132, 139
resources, 74, 79, 81, 84, 132
response, 10, 17, 18, 27, 33, 46, 61, 95, 102, 113, 116, 126, 128
restrictions, 23, 45, 55, 60, 133, 136, 138
restructuring, 86
retail, 33, 71, 74
retaliation, 28, 29
retirement, 91, 98, 100
revenue, 73

rights, 23
risk(s), x, 62, 64, 79, 81, 101, 105, 107, 108, 109, 116, 118, 119, 120, 126, 127, 140
rules, xi, 23, 24, 25, 28, 30, 32, 37, 54, 57, 131, 132, 134, 135, 137, 138, 139, 142, 143
Russia, viii, 2, 3, 9, 19, 36, 37, 88, 95

S

safe haven(s), xi, 13, 102, 109
safety, 99, 100
Saudi Arabia, 9, 36, 37, 95
savings, ix, 29, 42, 85, 86, 88, 89, 90, 91, 94, 100, 117, 126
savings account, 94
savings rate, 29
scope, 31
Secretary of the Treasury, 26, 55, 64
securities, ix, 42, 44, 76, 80, 99, 107, 108, 109, 110, 120, 122
security, 26, 107, 109
SED, 97
sellers, 120
seminars, 34
Senate, x, 18, 26, 33, 36, 39, 42, 43, 54, 57, 59, 63, 94, 97, 144
September 11, 129
services, x, 60, 73, 74, 77, 93, 102, 134, 135
shame, 56
shape, 6, 7, 25
shortfall, 72
short-term interest rate, 18, 77, 106
showing, 106
Singapore, 15, 27, 53, 68, 69
Slovakia, 34
social security, 85, 93
Social Security, 129
social welfare, 93
society, 75
solution, 83, 124, 129
South Africa, 36, 37
South Korea, 15, 19, 26, 27, 36, 37, 38, 88, 95
sovereignty, 78

Index

153

Spain, 34

speculation, 95, 111

speech, 129

spending, 25, 51, 75, 76, 77, 82, 85, 88, 89, 91, 93, 99, 112, 114, 119, 123, 126

spillover effects, 22

St. Petersburg, 19, 36, 38

stability, 22, 62, 78, 81, 94, 118, 120, 125, 136

stabilization, 123

state(s), x, 23, 24, 34, 54, 56, 73, 82, 93, 96, 97, 98, 99, 101, 123, 141

statistics, 33, 78, 95, 127, 128

statutory provisions, 26

steel, 80

stimulus, 18, 19, 51, 85, 93, 103, 117, 121, 123

stock, 108, 115

store of value, 118, 121

Strategic Economic Dialogue, 97

structural reforms, 19

Subsidies, 24, 37, 143

subsidy, ix, 24, 31, 42, 57, 58, 59, 61, 68, 80, 96, 135, 138, 139

substitutes, 34

surplus, 14, 50, 51, 56, 67, 70, 72, 79, 83, 89, 95, 104, 126, 127

surveillance, 23, 56, 66, 133, 134, 136, 141

sustainability, 66, 76, 129

Sweden, 68, 69

Switzerland, 12, 13, 14, 15, 17, 32, 53, 68, 69

T

Taiwan, 15, 26, 38, 53, 68, 69, 71

target, x, 8, 27, 65, 67, 101, 121, 123

tariff, 53, 80, 140, 141

taxes, 25, 140

technical assistance, 132

techniques, 59

technology, 46, 78

tension(s), 2, 32, 33, 43, 81

Thailand, 69, 95

theft, 84

threats, 19, 84

time periods, 111

TPA, 4, 22, 27, 30, 32, 33

trade agreement, 3, 4, 27, 30, 31, 43, 136, 140, 142

trade deficit, ix, 10, 12, 15, 25, 41, 43, 50, 54, 69, 70, 71, 72, 73, 75, 76, 77, 82, 83, 96, 98, 100, 104, 105, 112, 113, 125, 126, 128, 129

trade policy, 30, 44, 54

trade remedy, 57, 68

trading partners, ix, 14, 21, 26, 29, 41, 43, 49, 55, 59, 64, 81, 93

transactions, x, 7, 37, 62, 102, 104, 118, 133

transfer payments, 95

transparency, 30

transportation, 74

Treasury, xi, 4, 26, 28, 30, 34, 35, 37, 38, 55, 56, 57, 59, 60, 61, 66, 76, 96, 97, 102, 109, 110, 121, 122, 128, 129, 137, 139, 144

Treasury Secretary, 4, 26, 38, 60, 61, 129, 137, 139, 144

treatment, xi, 31, 132, 139, 141

Turkey, 36, 37

turnover, 108, 122

U

U.S. Bureau of Labor Statistics, 72

U.S. Department of Commerce, 127, 128

U.S. Department of Labor, 70

U.S. Department of the Treasury, 35, 38, 55, 100, 127, 128, 129

U.S. economy, ix, 2, 15, 16, 42, 44, 54, 57, 65, 69, 73, 74, 77, 82, 88, 99, 106, 112, 113, 114, 117, 121, 123, 124, 125

U.S. policy, viii, 2, 3, 50, 56, 65, 68

U.S. Treasury, viii, ix, 2, 22, 33, 42, 44, 76, 98, 99, 108, 109, 110, 144

UK, 6, 17, 21, 25

unemployment rate, 14, 76

uniform, 103

United Kingdom, 17, 36, 37, 88, 106, 108, 127

USA, 74, 129

V

valuation, 63, 115, 128, 141, 143
Valuation, 34
variables, 66
Vatican, 132
veto, 134
volatility, 64, 65, 119
vote, 58, 138, 142
voting, 23, 61

W

wages, 91, 93, 99, 100
waiver, 61, 135
war, vii, 1, 3, 10, 14, 18, 19, 34, 35, 121, 129
Washington, 37, 143
weak currencies, vii, viii, 1, 2, 10, 11, 29
weak currency, vii, viii, 1, 10, 11
weakness, 119
wealth, 19, 53, 77, 100

web, 127, 128
West Africa, 34
White House, 94, 97
wholesale, 74
worker rights, 91
workers, ix, 42, 46, 53, 54, 63, 71, 74, 78, 91, 98, 100
World Bank, 62, 84
World Trade Organization, xi, 22, 24, 37, 57, 60, 131, 132, 134, 143
World War I, 8, 24, 36
worldwide, 86, 89, 110
WTO, v, xi, 22, 24, 25, 28, 29, 32, 33, 37, 38, 57, 61, 63, 131, 132, 134, 135, 136, 137, 138, 139, 141, 142, 143, 144

Y

Yale University, 77
yield, 77, 106, 116
yuan, ix, 12, 13, 35, 41, 45, 46, 47, 48, 49, 78, 79, 83, 94, 95, 103, 119, 126